AS I HEARD SAY AND LIVED IT
- A LIFETIME

by

Eamon Carney

As I Heard Saw and Lived It - A Lifetime

Published in 2006 by Eamon Carney

ISBN
0-9554560-0-2
978-0-9554560-0-8

Printed in Ireland by Colour Books Ltd.

I dedicate my book to my wife, Pauline
for all her love, and care

Foreword

I am delighted to be asked to write a few words for Eamon on this excellent piece of work. I am honoured to oblige. This is a wonderful undertaking by Eamon and I am sure generations of people present and in the future will enjoy reading all about what it was like to live and work in rural Ireland. Eamon is covering a period of great change over the past 60 years. He recalls all about family life, social and cultural life, his neighbours, his school years and even when rural electrification arrived in the Parish. Who would believe that in the 40's and 50's there was no electricity in most of the country, very few cars or tractors and how family, neighbours and friends worked so well together and helped each other.

Eamon himself is a great tradesman like his father before him. I remember the desk in my mother's classroom in Ballicutranta National School, which she used all her teaching life, was made by Eamon's father, Andy, and given as a present to my late mother. I remember many a time sitting on that same desk during my school years there – my mother went to the same school and ended her teaching days there as Principal.

Eamon's excellent work can be seen in many houses and gardens throughout the area. He is a master builder and stonemason. Even during the time of his severe illness he kept going – it was the nature of the Carney Clan.

He is a great GAA man and has done wonderful work with all organisations in the Parish and the County – all of which are well covered in the book. He also found a lot of time to help me throughout my entire political career for which I will be forever grateful.

Eamon has produced a great read and a historical document, which I know, will give hours of joy to many people. It will help them understand the way things were and the progress that has been achieved over the past 60 years or so and the contribution he and his family have made in so many ways.

Well done and good luck.

Contents

Introduction

As one of the few senior locals who is totally in awe of our local area, and who only got the chance to appreciate it properly since I became partially disabled, I now have the time and the pleasure of writing my observations of the lives of my generation and before. But, with regret that I did not pay more attention to the stories of our forefathers.

As of now, rural Ireland is totally consumed with commercialisation and riches, never seen before and as a consequence, our heritage and all the country people's traditions are consigned to history, but not recorded because of the lightning pace of life in the twenty first century.

The ingredients of this book, as I am now in my sixties, have been flying through my head for some years. I've had a chequered career through work, sport, sickness and now Multiple Sclerosis. I am passionate about life as I lived it.

From memory I write, even though when MS struck me in the late nineteen eighties, I could not see the wood from the trees. Any article that I include from other sources is to verify my own story.

I know the younger generation might not read my story, but if they do, I promise they'll get a better insight into the overall picture of a lifetime. Without the help of modern aids, it is still possible to reflect back sixty years, with a total insight into this golden and intriguing world we live in.

I feel my generation lived in an era, which saw the greatest transformation the world has ever witnessed.

The chapters of these memoirs are sequenced from my life of the years of the 1940's, 50's, 60's, 70's, 80's, 90's to 2005. All articles as the title suggests, 'As I heard it, saw and lived it' through the lifetime of Eamon Carney and of the map area I include. The map is the very oldest I can procure of my area and is dated 1589.

This book also includes recitations, songs, photos, clichés, words and

Irish folklore. I hope my simple and fulfilled lifetime will give as much pleasure to the readers as it has given to me.

Finally, the names of the people I mention, who are both deceased and living are all mentioned with pride and honour and I acknowledge them all.

This is a photo taken of me as a young school boy

As I put the finishing touches to my book on this historic day, 1st October 2006, Sligo Gaelic Ladies Football Team are just after winning the Junior All Ireland Final in Croke Park. This is a huge credit to the girls and their management.

I talked to their goal keeper, Catriona Connolly two days previous of the final. She assured me of their confidence to achieve victory, which I am so proud to say they duly did. As I left her, I shook her hand and wished her and the team 'good luck'. Catriona's saves and her performance as 'Girl of the Match' speak volumes of her character and that of her team mates.

Eamon Carney

1

The War Years and the Plane Landing in 1941

I was born in 1942 when the Irish Republic was in its infancy and Ireland was still in the dark ages only twenty years after we gained our independence. Naturally I was born at home, as all children were at that time. My early memories are of my house – I was told many years later by its builder the cost of it, which was [1]£490.00 (old money) in 1935 – it was relatively new in the 40's. I remember its structure vividly. It had roof tiles with no underlay membrane. Ceiling boards inside, all through, which let in the draught and hailstones, which sometimes fell through the knotholes to the floor. The hearth fire opening was large, as was the chimney flue, which also let down the hailstones. The front and back doors had a space under them. The sash windows were also noisy and draughty. There was no electricity, no running water or sewage system, at this point in time. Still, everybody seemed happy and got on with life, and all '*as content as the flowers in May*'. . Incidentally, I still live in this house (but with additions and modifications) in an area of unspoiled scenery and beauty.

My father was part of the Army at the time and was involved in the Coast Watching Service from the lookout station at Aughris Head. The work was a twenty-four hour watch of that part of the Atlantic Ocean and about thirty miles of shoreline. The belief of the Intelligence Corps was that German forces would try and invade Ireland, even though it was declared a neutral country by Eamonn DeValera and the Government of the day.

The coast watching meant that the men who were watching through their binoculars could report to Army Headquarters on any irregular sightings, along with shipwrecks, or debris and bodies who were washed ashore. There were eight men in that Platoon. The phone connection consisted of a pair of wires on poles, a distance of three or four miles from Skreen Post Office to the lookout station, where the telephonist or postmistress plugged the call into Army Headquarters in Athlone.

I remember my father cycled eight miles to and from duty. In the springtime he also cycled to the bog afterwards, to cut and save the turf. The country was teeming with people, all who had simple living methods and made

---

[1] One would require EUR15.26 in July 2006 to have approximately the same purchasing power that (old) £1 had in 1970 - Central Bank & Financial Services Authority of Ireland

their own entertainment of Irish music, song, dance and storytelling. My father told me that there was a huge rapport among the coast watchers and the people of Aughris village, which, incidentally, no longer exists in village form, but the Beach Bar makes up for it with its international clientele and locally famous characters.

I remember a number of aircraft flying overhead and my father taught me to distinguish between them. The only name I remember now is the 'Flying Fortress'. He also taught me to decipher the 'Morse Code' and the nationality of ships flags as we had a chart hanging on the wall at home. It was hung beside a painting of 'The Tarter', which was the local ship ferrying goods between Sligo and Ballina. Towards the end of the war a plane force landed in Derk, a mile from my home. There was major excitement. They arrested the pilot, who, incidentally, was trying to get away from the war situation. After circling our area for an hour, they had pinpointed a large field in Derk, owned by John Michael Kilcullen. People told me afterwards that, as young boys at the time, they ran over hedges and ditches for miles to see the plane.

In 1990 I discussed this plane landing with John Higgins who, incidentally, was at the scene, as part of the LDF (Local Defence Force), when the army arrived. The civilians were pushed back, so that they could unload the bombs and make the scene safe. I was told that when the army men came to repair the plane they billeted in our out-office, as the big shed was known, at the time. The Officer in Charge stayed in our house and he was given his meals through the open window. The repair of the plane took six weeks and some of the army must have been Technicians and Engineers. Before the plane could be repaired they simply knocked the stone wall leading into the next field which was nearer to the road and was on higher ground to enable them build a runway for take-off. Incidentally, the field was owned by Peter Barrett. That was the only way out and they flew back to Baldonnell. I was told they circled our area as a gesture of farewell.

I still remember the restrictions we had throughout the war years. All my short travels to mass and visits to people's houses, were made by bicycle on the homemade timber seat that my father made for the carrier of my mother's bicycle. It was a simple timber made seat that fitted on the carrier of the bicycle. The verbal warning I got every time was *"Keep your feet well out from the spokes"*, as it happened, previously, that a child got his foot caught in the spokes with tragic consequences. My father made a seat for his bicycle. It proved to be a safer addition. It was attached to the crossbar of his bicycle and, when in position, I was safe between my father's arms and the handlebars. I remember those times perfectly, as I scoot along those same roads in my retirement on my electric scooter in glorious sunshine.

My Father's Diary Entry of my Birth

2

The Drowning Tragedy of 1944

I remember the first major tragedy that occurred in Portavade, adjacent to the townland where I was born and have lived in all my life. It happened in 1944 on the 28th of August. This is something no toddler should be able to recall, but maybe the reason I can is because it was recalled in my presence so many times. Where I live along the Ballisadare Bay and Peninsula, which is incidentally, seven miles long from Ballisadare Village to the broad Atlantic to where the Blackrock Lighthouse is the beacon for ships going into Sligo Harbour. Across from our shore to Strandhill is still quite a short journey, only two miles across, but it is eighteen miles to travel by road through the village of Ballisadare.

As life was coming into the forties motor transport was just starting. Only the priest and the doctor could employ the only hackney car that was owned by John McMunn of Beltra. I remember in the late forties my father hired it to take my mother and myself to Strandhill for the day to visit friends. At the time horse racing was held on Culleenamore Strand, in Strandhill with all the Fun Fair and Amusements that were available then. The amusement consisted of ring throwing over objects with the contestant spaced, maybe, 10ft. away and if you were successful your prize was the ornament or object that your rubber ring sat neatly over. It was impossible to perfect your ring throwing without frustration and consequently, you spent more money buying rings to throw and compete, to try and get them to sit down over the square wooden block that the object was sitting on.

Swinging boats was another attraction, also, the rifle range. Naturally, every young fellow fancied his shot. Sheaf throwing was another event that attracted the strong young fellows. Wheat or oats had to be pitched with a pitch fork over a bar that was attached to two vertical poles, maybe 15ft. high with a crossbar, which was raised by a rope as each competitor perfected the height, until the fellow that could throw the sheaf the highest won the competition. Other events were the fortune tellers and 'trick-of-the-loubes' of all sorts, plus the main attraction which was the horse racing. Naturally, for the teenage boys from our shore it was an absolutely brilliant day's fun. They also waited for the dance that night in the Plaza Ballroom to round it off.

My next-door neighbours Michael Patrick Kilcullen and his brother Martin owned a boat of, maybe 15ft. to 20ft. long, big enough to take approximately six people. And sure enough, there was no shortage of passengers, too many as it turned out. A few were disappointed including Pauline Tempany, Ardagelly, Templeboy - Phil Dooney, Skreen - Joe O'Brien, Leekfield and Jimmy and Mabel Kearins, Bunnina.

At the time it was easy to hear the sound of music being played across the water from our shore, which was tempting in itself and to be part of the enjoyment of it all. Coming home in the bright light of the next morning the boat, which was loaded with revellers (two fellows walked the twenty miles by road – Jimmy Kenny and Henry Farry) as bad luck had it, tragedy struck what turned out to be an ill-fated journey. The wind got up and the sail was impossible to undo, so all capsized into the choppy water with no lifesaving equipment. Six young men were tragically drowned, and their names were as follows; Michael Patrick Kilcullen, aged 21 years and his brother Martin, aged 19 years from Carrowflatley, Dromard. Thomas Battle aged 20 years from Ballyferris, Templeboy. Muredach Foley aged 18 years from Carrownaknockan, Skreen. Thomas Flynn, aged 37 years from Carrowcaslan, Skreen. Edward (Bertie) Neary, aged 40 from Carrowmorris, Dromard.

To this day I can recall it without knowing why. I was only two years old. I still think I remember playing with turkeys' prepared food on Sarah Kilcullen's floor, as my father and mother gave the family moral support or as much as was humanly possible in the circumstances. The whole neighbourhood searched the shoreline day and night until the sea gave up all the bodies - at our landing point, at Portavade, and across the bay in Strandhill, at Raughley near Maugherow and Streemstown near Ballisadare, before the six young men were laid to rest.

The following extract was taken from the Western People of 2nd September 1944

> 'On Tuesday afternoon a rudder and an oar were found by Dan Farry, Bunnina, Skreen, near the spot where the boat was found on Monday. Some time later a man's soft hat was found which was identified as belonging to the missing Bertie Neary.
>
> The two Kilcullen boys were the eldest sons and sole support of their widowed mother who has six younger children, three of whom are still of school-going age. One of the sons (PJ) had been in England and returned recently. One of her daughters is employed at the Grand Hotel, Sligo'.

My Father's Diary Entry of the Tragedy

A Poem to commemorate the tragedy was written by Mary Finnegan of Templeboy and reads as follows;

The banshee is cooing o'er the hedge row and glen,
As Tireragh is mourning six gallant young men.
Struck down in their prime a sailing for home,
When the wee craft foundered beneath the blue foam.

In the springtime of life, they've gone to their rest,
Leaving old friends and family who are sorely distressed.
In the dawn of the morning, they pulled to the shore,
Which alas and alack they'll never see more.

No more on the headland their laughter and song,
These loving companions they wandered along,
They strolled in the morning at the dawn of the day,
And watched the sun setting on fair Sligo Bay.

Requescant them in Pace is all we can say,
That God in His Goodness will fondly pray.
That He in his mercy will give their souls rest,
'Till we join in high heaven with friends we love best.

Commemorative Window in Skreen Church

3

Compulsory Tillage and the Big Snow of 1947

1939-45 were known as the *'emergency years'* and farmers were forced to be more industrious regards tilling their land and the Sligo Champion of 12th January 1946 had the following notice.

Good news for farmers - Mr. John Greer, the popular Skreen businessman, has now added another enterprise to his thriving business. He has procured a new tractor plough and will be ready to undertake ploughing operations for the coming year. An experienced ploughman (Bertie Uncles) *has been engaged to take charge of the plough.*

As we were still in the aftermath of the Second World War, in the following years our Government of the time brought in a law of Compulsory Tillage, whereby each large farm owner was compelled to till 25% of their land. My memory was of seeing the large farm of Carna Gloc, which is across the road from my house, and which contains 130 acres approximately, of which 25 or 30 acres were tilled. As a young boy, it was amazing to see the start of the mechanical era and smell the tractors T.V.O. fuel. That was what was used before diesel. Also, it was gradually replacing horsepower. The Cuffe family, who owned the machinery, stored it in my father's yard.

Another memory for me of the compulsory tillage era was seeing the party for the agricultural workers in my house at the end of the harvest of '46. The Farm owner, Jimmy Kilgallon, bought a barrel of Guinness in reward for a job well done. I remember my father nailing ceiling boards at elbow height on our sash windows. It was to prevent glass breakages as fellows neared the bottom of the barrel of Guinness. That was an extra bonus.

The tillage at the time was potatoes, oats, wheat, mangles and turnips. The farm owner who was, Jimmy and Art Kilgallon, owned a 'Baby Ford', and I remember, one day, Jimmy's feet went through the floor of it due to its old rusty condition.

Notices Posted in the Sligo Champion at the time

HOW FARMERS CAN HELP

A great many farmers have been enquiring as to whether there is anything they, as individuals, could do to help the Government.

THE ANSWER IS—YES

If every tillage farmer in Ireland will:—

1.—FAITHFULLY COMPLETE HIS COMPULSORY TILLAGE QUOTA.

2.—SOW FROM ONE TO FIVE ACRES EXTRA OF BARLEY OR OATS.

He will honestly help the Government and the Nation.

Every farmer's wife who SELLS an EXTRA hundred of eggs to the egller will help materially, too.

I believe co-operation works better than compulsion.

LET'S SHOW THEM !!

JAMES M. DILLON,
Minister for Agriculture.

POTATOES

A regrettable feature in our tillage during the emergency was the absence of any material increase in the potato crop.

The present improved fertiliser supplies should enable us to overcome the greatest obstacle to potato production.

Potatoes are of great importance, both as human food and feeding for animals. They provide a reserve store of food and are our second line of defence against want.

The new production scheme will greatly increase the value of poultry on the farm. Pig and cattle production also offers good returns. For all these classes of stock, potatoes are a valuable and easily produced feeding stuff.

There will also be an export market for any potatoes which are produced in excess of our requirements.

Every farmer should, therefore, take steps to increase his production of potatoes this year.

The sprouting of an adequate supply of tubers should be put in hands at once for early planting. The planting of whole sprouted certified seed as early as the season permits will contribute towards greater production, but to provide a substantially increased output a considerable extension in the area under potatoes is required.

(Issued by the Department of Agriculture.)

In 1947, we had the biggest snowfall of the Century. It drifted onto the roadways and blocked the only transport - bread vans, hearse and horse transport. As it was so powdery, dry and deep, the local farm force and young fellows were organized by Sligo County Council to shovel a 6ft. path through it. The big snow lasted for six weeks. I often listened to the jovial side of the workers about fellows cutting the snow in blocks and sometimes building obstructions in front of contrary people's entrances.

I heard a story about one girl who decided she could shovel the snow, as the pay was nearly £1 old money, for an eight hour day. One day she got short-taken, there was no toilet; she sat behind a bush, as she thought, out of view. One of the fellows said to his fellow workers that she *"was a man, who had the arse worked off herself"*. The snow did not melt away until the month of May and it sure was hardship. I remember being able to look down my neighbour's chimney because of the drifts accumulated on the road in front of John Gilligan's house. Some animals died and I saw rats running from the side of a dead cow of ours, incidentally, the only one we had. That was the year that I started National School.

An Article in the Sligo Champion at the time gave similar accounts of the blizzard in all parts of the county. The piece relating to my area read as follows;

DEEP DRIFTS AT SKREEN

'Drifts from ten to twelve feet deep were to be found in the Dromard and Skreen district and traffic was held up by impassable roads. County Council workers were engaged in clearing the main road and the first mails for a week were delivered on Tuesday'.

4

Memories of My Father and His
Sudden Death in 1955

My Account of his death in his Diary

My father's death was sudden for my mother and myself, as I was only eleven years old. I was in the kitchen preparing onions for setting in the garden on the evening he died. He simply dropped his head as he read the Irish Press after eating his dinner. I heard a snore and I thought he was asleep but it was the conclusion of his life.

He always kept a diary record of every day of his life - where he was working, how much things cost etc. He died on the 5th April 1955 and his diary was written up to the 4th April. After the funeral, I recovered it and the first thing I entered was the time he died; who came in; and the cars that were at his funeral. As he was an Army Veteran, an Army Platoon fired a volley of shots over his coffin as it was being lowered into the grave. I have been told lately, that I said a decade of the Rosary in Irish at the graveside with his army medals pinned to my coat. It was on Easter Sunday, which is still very much in people's minds since the troubles of 1916 -- 1922.

I remember my father's very republican belief and his total honour for the 'Tricolour' – the *'Green, White and Gold'* flag. It was erected on a flag pole at each of the two memorial Celtic crosses in the vicinity of Beltra to his comrades, Tommie Goff and Paul Geoghegan, both of whom were shot by the *'Black and Tans'*. I remember being with my father at the erection of those crosses. The Tricolour was also flown for the duration of Holy Week. I carried on that tradition for some years after my father's death, but as I grew up I realised that it was best not to portray any symbolism as we had entered very different times. It was best to let our elected representatives deal with any volatile and sensitive issues of the day.

The reason why my father called me 'Eamon' was because of his admiration for Eamon DeValera, the leader of the Irish Republic, who had played a big part in the formation of the State. But, alas, when a neighbour and good friend, who was an opponent of the Treaty and of a totally different viewpoint to 'Dev' heard who Andy (my father) had called his son after, he exclaimed and said, *"Could 'Andien' call the son any other name only after the 'oul b******!"* Such was the bitterness that prevailed which our young people now know nothing about.

Our parents were also very concerned that we learn proper manners and know how to behave in public. Some of the regimental things he impressed on me were - "Walk straight and upright and lightly swing your arms." "When someone shakes hands with you, always reciprocate by giving a warm handshake and always look them in the face." "Always sit properly on a chair." "Always ride your bicycle in an upright position." "Never put your shoe on a chair when tying your laces."

My mother was a great and compassionate woman and kept me encouraged at all farm and garden jobs after he died. The day after his funeral, it was time to put down the onions that I had been preparing on the evening of his death and the *'early york'* cabbage plants that he had brought home on the carrier of his BSA motorbike. I remember the motorbike well. It was a green one. And the number of it was EI 5739. My mother sold it soon after his death, together with his guns, as she was afraid I might ride the motorbike, shoot with the guns and end up killing myself.

At my father's funeral I remember the piece of black velvet cloth, approximately 3" by 2" that my mother had sewn, in a diamond formation, on the left sleeve of my coat. And, I also had a black tie and a white shirt. It was the symbol of mourning for each and every male member of the family, and they also wore it for twelve months of mourning. People also refrained from attending dance halls and all forms of entertainment as a matter of respect. I vividly remember a person that went to a dance six months after their mother had died, and they were the talk of the place.

After his death, which was startling for an eleven year old, selling and buying a few cattle was for the experienced and trusted, namesake farmer, John Carney RIP, who offered his services. The plan was that I would be at his side to learn the trade and be well able to stand up to all the 'tanglers' who were always looking to buy or sell a cheap animal. I remember selling a heifer for £47 old money, and the money just paid for my father's headstone and I made the kerbing.

Headstone Receipt from 1962

The fair in Farnaharpy was always on the 27th of every month and a major day in the farming community within a 25-mile radius. We also had to go with cattle to Collooney fair. This was a 3 o'clock in the morning start, as we had a journey of twelve miles. The reason for the early start was to allow cattle buyers to buy our cattle with flash lamps and send them by train to Enniskillen and then on to Belfast for the boat for, either, Scotland or England. The train left Collooney at 8 o'clock each morning. One thing I remember was that our cattle buyer spent more on replacing our stock and he always maintained the importance of keeping up the value of the stock on the land. But, it also meant that the margin of profit was almost nil. My good mother received a widow's pension which amounted to £1.10 shillings, old money. She also had our local National School Teacher, Miss Duffy, staying which also supplemented the income.

A memory of my young days saving turf on the bog was seeing a Pipe and Drum Band marching and playing and maybe fifty men with turf spades on their shoulders. They were on their way to cut turf on a certain bog, which they hoped the Land Commission would take possession of and hand to them. I will never forget seeing the same large group of men trouncing back by my turf bank in about an hour's time, because of the heaviest rain I ever saw, which had disrupted their plans.

My memory is of myself and John Niland still working, but that made up John's mind for him. The work ethic at the time, in the fifties, was to make the most of the day's work on the bog, as the journey was long, at least five miles over the mountain, and we had no motorized transport. Incidentally, Johnny was cutting the turf and I was spreading them. I placed twelve or fifteen neatly and horizontally on the barrow, then wheeled them to the '*spread ground*', and gently slid them off. I was only thirteen or fourteen at the time. This was life in the '50's. Still, we had great fun and enjoyed the lovely warm, slightly windy days. All scribes recall those days, the special taste of the tea, the boiled eggs, the soda bread, the homemade butter and the strawberry jam.

One day, my cousin, Tommy Carney, who had a sheep dog called, 'Jess', came to give us a hand. But, I'm afraid Jess was no help. She got to where we had our lunch bags hidden in the bog hole and ate most of what we had for an our tea break. Hungry days are bad days, and as my good neighbour, Paddy, used to say, *"A full bag will not bend and an empty one will not stand up"*, and I remember the latter being the case on that day.

The turf season also included scattering, footing, re-footing in bad summers and putting the turf out to the side of the road and building them in a neat stack. Each man was very proud of his stack of turf. It was lovely to look round at all the stacks along all the network of roads for miles around on Cabra Bog. Bringing them home in the month of September was another big day. I was fortunate to live in the '50's, as a motor lorry had arrived just then. There was no hydraulic tipping that time, but Michael James Feeney, from Derk, was classified as a *'God-send'.* Imagine being able to fill five or six ton of turf onto the lorry and have all the years supply home in three journeys.

I also remember my father built a big turf shed for them before he died. Imagine the step forward – no need to rebuild the turf into a stack in the yard. The fact that the turf was dry when my mother went to get a basket of them was wonderful.

Cutting large trees for firewood was all the go at the time, as well. I remember seeing two men with a large crosscut saw, sawing over and back for, maybe, two hours, until the tree fell in the appointed direction. There was a lot of skill involved in felling a tree, if we were lucky to acquire one. When it was lying horizontally, the big work started. The branches had to be sawn off and then the repeat of cross cutting, maybe 18 or 22 inches long, depending on the size of your fireplace. Whenever they were required for paling posts they were cut at lengths of 5 or 6 feet, and all lengths had to be split with steel wedges and the hatchet, which was also used for splitting firewood, and the branches to be used as firelighters. If they were going to the sawmill, depending on quality, the length might be 14 or 15 feet. There was no chainsaw in my days and keeping the home fires burning was a very important part of the year's work, soon after my father's death.

My Father in his uniform of the time

My Parents on their Wedding Day with Bridesmaid, Julia Maye (her sister) and Best Man, Sgt. Paddy Coffey

TELEPHONE NUMBERS		MEMORANDA FROM 1941
Name	**Number**	

Telephone Numbers:

Name	Number
Aughris Head Skreen	8
Hazlewood	212
Easkey Lendoon	4
Clifferey Mullaghmore	5
Ballysull Roskeragh	3
Skreen Barrack	2 R
Dromore West	3 R3
Drumcliff Creamary	48
Castle Bar	91
athlone	14
Hospital Sligo	2
Castlepollard	6
County Home	4
A.T. Gallagher Collooney	

Memoranda from 1941:

Paid For Labour £ s d
in 1941 — 22.19.6

Hay Potatoes Barly Wheat 3. 14.

Rent Rates and Bog 11. 17. 6

Eand of 1941. £38.11.0

got all Plough Done
By J Underwood 20 March

Put Down Early Potatoes
4 of April and the Onions

Oats & Potatoes 9th April

I tarry finished the Lief
27 April.

Soed the Crean and
Lettes Seed 24 April

Scatered Turf 2nd May

Futting 7 & 9 May

My Father's Diary showing the telephone numbers relevant to him regarding his coast watching duties. Note County Home 6 is now St. John's Hospital. Also recorded is his Bookkeeping for the farm.

5

My Mother's Lifetime

Like all young girls of her generation, work came first for their meagre survival. School years were very limited, and she secured her first job at the age of fourteen. Her job was to train as a Cook in the local Longford House Estate. Sir Henry Crofton and his family were to be her employers for the next few years. Naturally, it was all *'Upstairs, Downstairs'* at the time. All the workers on the estate had a certain status, from the Chief Steward who laid out the work, to the horsemen, cattlemen, gardeners, butlers, cooks and the maids.

Later, when my mother went to New York, this experience stood to her. Even though she was only sixteen years old, she obtained secure employment with a well-to-do family, as their cook. She used to tell me all about the 'underworld', as she had a near escape with death. Apparently, she worked for the Gallo Family, of Italian descent, who had connections with the *'underworld'*. Mr. Gallo was a Boxing Manager for Primo Canearo, Champion of the World in 1931. When he called to the Manager's house he had to be served two portions of dinner. He used to praise Mary-Ellen Maye (my mother) and often gave her a tip. She had a photograph taken with him. He was a huge man, 6'.11" in height. She had some very happy years working for the Gallo family.

But, one night, all hell broke loose when the house was raided by a number of men with guns. They came to shoot Mr. Gallo. But he must have got a tip-off and he was not at home. They tied up his two daughters, who were in the house. But they did not tie up the young Irish girl, with the red hair. I suppose they knew that she was not Italian.

Another story my mother told me was about the kidnapping of a child of the famous aviator, Charles Lindbergh, who had just acquired world notoriety following his successful completion of the first transatlantic flight in 1927. The prize for his great accomplishment was $25,000, a huge sum of money at the time. As a result of his fame, his son was kidnapped for ransom. My mother told me how after the kidnapping, she had seen the ladder still up to the window of the Lindbergh house where it had been left.

My six children knew her well and all the stories of her life. Pauline benefited from her experience in cooking and the routines of household duties which she has combined with her duties as a nurse until my mother's death in 1979.

My father knew her before she went to America and used to send her a copy of the 'Sligo Champion' every few weeks, but she told him she would not marry him unless he moved from his mountain home and build a new house. This he did and finally persuaded her to get married on her return to Ireland for the Eucharistic Congress in 1932, even though, she was engaged to a German man. She went back to the United States to work for four more years. She eventually came back to Beltra in 1936, *'bag and baggage'*, and sent her engagement ring to her boyfriend's sister in New York. But until the day she died, she was fearful of him locating her, and was always watchful of American visitors, folks she always enjoyed entertaining when they visited us. The end of the story is that it was six more years before their only child (*myself*) was born.

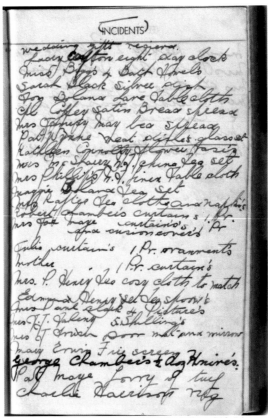

Copy Diary Entry showing Wedding Gift List

My Mothers Wedding Gifts in 1935

Lady Crofton	An Eight Day Clock
Miss Biggs	Four Bath Towels
Sarah Black	A Silver Dish
Tom Boland	A Lace Table Cloth
Sergeant Coffey	A Satin Bed Spread
Mrs. Johnny Maye	Bed Spread
Pat Wynne	Meat Dishes and Glasses
Kathleen Connolly	Flower Vases
Mrs. McSharry NT	China Tea Set (Still here and very proud and lovely)
Mrs. Philips NT	A Fine Lemon Tablecloth
Maggie Boland	A Tea Set
Mrs. Rafter	A Tea Cloth and Napkins
Robert Chambers	A Pair of Curtains
Mrs. Joe Maye	A Pair of Curtains and Cushion Covers
Julia (Her Sister)	A Pair of Ornaments and Curtains
Mother	A Pair of Curtains
Mrs. P Henry	A Tea Cosy and Cloth to match
Edmund Henry (still alive and hale and hearty)	A Set of Tea Spoons
Mrs. Paul Clarke	Four Pictures
Mrs. John Joe Taheny	Five Shillings
Mrs. J ----------	A Door Matt and Mirror
Mary Irwin	A Fire Screen
George Chambers	A Half Dozen Knives
Pat Maye	A Lorry of Turf
Charlie Harrison	A Rug
Mary Henry	Two Pillow Slips
Mrs. Lilly Martin	A Bed Spread
Mrs. Savage	3 Pullets (young hens)
Mrs. Crighton	Basket and 2 Candle Sticks
Mrs. Kelly NT	Tray Cloth
Mrs. Talbott	Two Lace Scarves

Photo of my mother and myself with my cousin Karen from America and our trusty dog 'Moss' and the cat, all around the fireside.

My mother and I at my cousin, Mary Teresa Harrison's wedding in 1964. She married Harry Collery and they are living in Dublin.

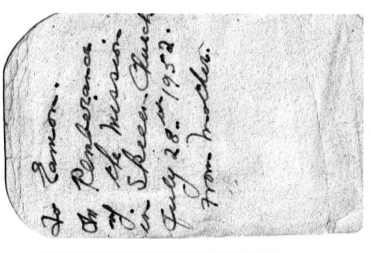

I still have the holy picture given to me by my mothr in remembereance of Skreen mission 1952

6

My Good Neighbours

When I reflect on my good neighbours I remember the sense of unity we had. Each of my neighbours gave my mother and myself total help at all yearly chores including the vegetable garden, saving turf, saving hay, oats and potatoes and maintaining stone walls and hedges. Their names I recall with pride Paddy Finneran, and Michael Boland who lived one each side of our house and never let us down even though the pay was only £1, old money, per day.

Michael was an institution round our house. He was an ex-army man who came to live next door to us. Himself and his Irish speaking wife and family moved to our neighbourhood from Gweedore, in Donegal. They were a wonderful family who fitted in superbly with us. Mary knitted Aran cardigans and was also a very religious person. The family all said the Rosary in Irish. The big problem they encountered was not being able to translate their confessions to English. This they soon overcame and able to tell the priest their harmless misdemeanours. After Mary died, Michael told me that when his time came he wanted to be buried with Mary in Gweedore and he wanted me to place his hurley on his coffin. Many's a time I chided him that we weren't going to waste a day going down to Gweedore with him and that he'd have to be buried in Dromard like the rest of us. Michael was very insistent that he be buried with his wife in Gweedore. When the time came, I was proud to make the journey to Gweedore and grieve with his family and friends, where I carried out his request and placed his hurley on the coffin.

Then we had Peter Kilgallon 'Sonny' as we knew him who always tended to sick animals and was equal to the vet; 'Dommie' Kilcawley who was the handy man, cut our hair and repaired our bicycles as well; Dan Farry the man who brought the milk to the Creamery and tilling. (Big) Michael Kilcullen also came if we needed extra strength – he was almost seven feet tall. As my mother's creamery can was the first to be collected, it meant she had to have the milk ready to be collected at seven o'clock. Even though she sent milk to the creamery, she was still able to give a bottle of milk to the neighbours each side of us and still have some to keep for churning and making butter. The skim milk she got returned from the creamery was fed to two calves and a pig – a bit like the *'loaves and fishes'*!

My other dependable good neighbour was Maureen Kearins. Herself and Pat had a phone before any of us. That was the house to go to if there was an emergency. Maureen would drive us anywhere. Maureen was one of the greatest people I ever knew and a Pioneer all her life.

The Rambling house of Tommy Doherty was an important place for the neighbours to go at night. I recall it vividly as I went there as a young boy with my father. It was there that Tommy discussed with the ramblers all the world issues plus the laws of the time. Even as a child I can recall the conversations. I would equate it to the present day T.V. programme 'Questions & Answers.' I remember one intelligent man who used to cycle six or seven miles, once or twice a week to Doherty's; his name was John McGrath – I remember the discussion one night was on strong men and the local man, Joe O'Brien, who could carry five hundred weight (5 cwt) at a time up to a grain loft, which was up a stone stairs to the second floor. I remember the conclusion of a night's chat in Doherty's when John McGrath said that in years to come a machine would be invented that would be able to that job. He also said that each generation was getting weaker and that in seven generations time (this was the early 1950s) it would take seven men to pull up a '*buchalain*' (ragwort weed).

My Father always brought me rambling on a Friday night as I had not to get up for school next morning and that was education in itself. The rambling would continue until two or three o'clock with the ghost stories always towards the end of it. Even Tommy had to be up at seven o clock each morning to tackle his horse and cart and get away to work – Tommy was before his time, as it were.

Next door Paddy Finneran was our *'right-hand man'* when our garden, tillage, hay, hedges and walls had to be tended to. Paddy is the man who taught me all I knew about building dry stone walls etc., and farmwork, which we diligently did at their set time each year. He was very conscientious and scolded me for not giving it my full attention. He used to say to me that I would *"never be good for nothing"*. I would answer him and say *"That's great, Paddy! I'll be good for something so!"*

I'm glad to say that Paddy's grandson, Keith, has done him proud in the Special Olympic 2006, in Belfast where he won Gold in the 100mt Sprint and Silver in the Shot Putt. (Well done Keith!)

Keith Finneran and myself at his celebratory reception
upon his return home from victory at the Special Olympics

The tradition of the townland station is still a worthy and neighbourly occasion for everyone to pray and attend Mass in a rotation of homes around every parish. I was proud to have this photograph taken of my family with our Parish Priest, Fr. Michael O'Horo, on the occasion of our most recent Area Station in 2005.

This photo was taken of my family during our Area Station
Included from left to right are - David & Deirdre Williams with my two grandchildren
Sadbh and Daragh Williams, Paul Carney, Niamh Carney, Fr. Michael O'Horo (Parish
Priest), Sinead Carney, Fiona Carney, Eimear Carney, Pauline and myself.

1

My School Years – Ballinleg and Easkey

Ballinleg National School was built in 1846. If you can imagine one big classroom full of long seats and benches with a Slate and 'Glantóir', (that was a piece of cloth that was used by the pupils to 'wipe their slates clean'). The Slate and Glantóir were kept on the shelf under each bench. Those benches also had inkwells for the pupils to dip their nib pens and to write all copybook lessons. The headlines were pre-done on the copybook and it was a major job to try and write in similar style. Blots were torture and always got on your copy.

Actually, the rats had a good time under the floor. Bread, even though it was scarce, was not always eaten but thrown away, so it attracted rats. My school had not the luxury of even a *'dry toilet'*, except one for the teacher. We were lucky that there was no school boundary, as the school was built in the corner of the farm, and gorse bushes were growing nearby, which gave good privacy at toilet times. Windows were broken and drafty as were the doors. The porch with the only external door was also the cloakroom - imagine, a few nails holding thirty or forty coats.

The first pupils to school in the morning had the best chance of their coat staying on the nails. But the problem was for the younger pupils, when they rushed to go home at two o'clock, coats fell all over the place. It was some job for the young pupils to get their coats, as they had to root through the pile on the floor to get their own one. No doubt, my generation has the same stories to tell as all schools have in the country. Every pupil had to bring a sod of turf, or the father who could afford it for his own family, brought a cart of turf, to ensure some heat during the winter.

One family, the Leydons, lived about six miles from our school. They used to travel by ass and cart. It was handy sometimes for me to get a lift in, if it was not too packed with children. The donkey was let graze in a neighbour's field, owned by the James family, near the school, during school hours. But then, low and behold, didn't Jimmy Kearins buy a 'Baby Ford', and Jimmy sometimes brought us to school in it, if it was raining. He would bring me with his own family if he was not attending a fair.

The next major event during my national school years was in 1949. We moved into a big, new, one-roomed school, with dry toilets (which, incidentally, was a small scoop of clay instead of the flush toilets of today). We also had a play shelter, and a good, flat playground to play football on.

The school was lovely and bright with a timber floor, two-seater desks and a wall-mounted blackboard (Even though the teacher brought the old blackboard and easel stand with her from the old school.)

It also had a solid fuel stove with a fireguard. It mainly left the teacher warm, but the teacher was generous, (as she thought), because she let us warm our milk bottles around it. Naturally, the corks had to be removed before the heat was applied, but still, the bottles of milk were warm on one side. The eldest of the Kearins family, Dympna, (now Mrs. Francie Rooney, of Glencar) was my minder at school.

My personal experience of the milk bottle was letting it fall out of my school bag on the first morning we moved to the new school. The bottle hit the iron frame of the seat and broke on the new floor. That was in 1949 and I was in first class and it sure christened the school.

As the numbers grew in the new one-roomed school, the classroom proved too small. But the thinking of the Manager and the Inspector was to employ a new Assistant Teacher. As the school had only one room, the next bright idea they came up with was to have a teacher teach at both ends of the classroom. This did not prove too successful, as both teachers and pupils had to shout louder to be heard.

After a few months of mayhem, the next idea that came to the teachers was to convert the cloakroom into another classroom for the second teacher and the infant pupils. The classes rotated, had a makeshift carpet of brown woven material, laid on the red tile floor, and they also installed an oil heater – all for comfort. But, the fumes from the 'tall green heater', proved overcoming for us little ones. The idea of an open container of water on its top, was to suggest that the fumes would disappear. This system prevailed until I left National School in 1956.

Back in 1952 when our school acquired the new teacher, she stayed in our house, which left life uncomfortable for me, especially around homework time. She was a lovely young girl of nineteen, and her name was Marcella Duffy of Ballinagar, Co. Roscommon, but, to me, she was old. She is now Mrs. Noel Cavanagh. Shyness prevailed and I used to hide my homework jotter and schoolbooks under my lumber jacket, and take a de-tour to my neighbour's house for her to help me.

Picture of Ballinlig School today with its beautiful Batik Art which was created by the pupils in 1999/2000

The neighbour's name was 'Mary McMunn', and I called her 'Munn'. I could not let Miss Duffy see me, as she might not like it. I was average at most things at school, but Geography was my favourite. I loved drawing maps of countries, especially Ireland. I thought it was a puppy with Achill as its short paws, and Wexford as its short tail, and Lough Neagh representing its ears – all in my eyes.

Learning Catechism was our first introduction to religion, even though the Rosary and Prayers were recited every night with my mother. Then, we all knew about Adam and Eve, Cain and Abel and that God made the world. We all graduated to long Catechism and the Bible History. This was big stuff, as we had to have it off by heart for the Religious Examiner, who came to our school once a year. I remember one time when Dr. McDonald, who incidentally, became Bishop of Kilalla later, asked one boy in our class to say *'Grace After Meals'.* He was 'gob-smacked'. Naturally, the priest asked him what his mother says when she has her dinner eaten. The boy replied, *"Oh! she says, Thanks be to God. Me belly is ready to burst".* That excuse caused a bit of frustration on the teacher's face. Another boy was asked why he was not at school the day before, and he said he could not come because his *'tag'* (a short jacket) was wet.

It was important to know all the answers for the religious examiner as we were told that the Bishop would not confirm us if we did not answer correctly. The worst thing we were told was that the Bishop would give us a slap on the side of our face, as Confirmation was about making us 'true Christians'.

I was an only child and my cousins, the Harrison family, would come from Ballisadare for their summer holidays to my house. We all played together. But, one day at the 'Angelus', when I could not pronounce 'Pray for us sinners' properly, my cousin, Mary Teresa, mocked me and said, *"Oh! He's praying for his dinner".* No doubt, that interrupted the Angelus and we ended up on the grass outside, with me pulling her two long plaits. At the Rosary at night, all young people were prone to giggling, especially if a bang happened or a mouse ran across the floor.

While still remembering the 1950's, each and every young person could not go out at night without joining in the Rosary. I often had to join in a second Rosary, when I called to Kearin's for Mícheál, if the Rosary was still on. Mabel and Jimmy, who had huge 'trimmings', had to have all answered properly. Then, the nightlife could start, which was not always compatible to home life. Still, when I look back, it was a simple and uncomplicated life, even with no cigarettes or alcohol. My main reason for illustrating all about my school days and my young life is that, maybe, young people will compare it with their present-day luxurious lifestyle and how complicated life is at the moment.

In 1956, it was time for me to leave National School. My mother always wanted me to learn a trade, but, our cattle buyer told her, *"not to be foolish. Wasn't there plenty of work round the country with the farmers"* for me and, anyway I would *"learn too much devilment at a strange school"*. How and ever, my mother had her way and sent me to Easkey Vocational School at the age of twelve or thirteen, and still in short trousers. I was one of three boys who still wore short trousers when starting the 'Tec' - Sean Sweeney and T J Finan were the other two. This was real education for me. The big boys were rough and tough, and the girls were lovely and petite. We went the sixteen miles from Dromard to Easkey by bus in the wintertime, and the weekly ticket cost nine shillings and three pence - a third of my mother's weekly widow's pension. When the good weather came in spring, all the boys and girls would cycle to the 'Tec'. Vincie McHugh and myself had the furthest to cycle. One night when practising for a play, I had to cycle home in the worst snowstorm that I ever remember. There was no way I could be persuaded to stay in the adjoining hotel, as I had to get home to my widowed mother, as there were no phones that time from which I could ring her to ease her mind.

Before I started my cycling days, my cousin, Tommy, bought me a new 'Humber' bicycle. I remember it cost £15 old money. There were no gears on it, but it had a dynamo which was very encouraging, because, the faster you cycled the better the light would get.

Woodwork, Mechanical Drawing; Rural Science; Bookkeeping; English; Irish and Maths were taught there. But, football was 'No 1' with us. At our pitch at the 'Tec', the surface was ok. But, we had no goal posts. So, my cyclist classmates and myself purchased four twenty foot high forestry poles at Fergus's Shop in Dromore West, one morning. We transported them with us – one cyclist front and rear per post, the five miles, to the consternation of everybody who saw us, especially Fr. Brady who came upon us at Conlon's Corner, a ninety degree corner which left the road too narrow for us and Fr. Brady's Morris Minor. Consequently we got knocked from our bicycles and Fr. Brady simply said, *"Aren't ye the Ludurmauns"* (fools). Eventually, to our satisfaction we arrived at our destination and erected them. We had some wonderful years playing football. We played it before class, at lunch breaks, and in the evening before bus time. Teams were selected for the County Championship during class. Dermot Conlon, who was my classmate, a native of Skreen, was the biggest amongst us, and was great for protection. I always kept in with the big boys and also the good footballers. In fact, Aidan Caffrey won an All Ireland Vocational Championship in 1957 and he was a classmate of ours at the time.

Picture from Sligo Champion of Vincie McHugh with myself and Pauline taken at the Tubbercurry Fair Day in July '06 – fifty years on.

Devilment was never too far away from our minds, and we hid each other's bicycles, put wrong items in schoolbags, and one fellow even nailed a woodwork block plane to the bench with a 6" nail, only to draw the worst explicatives from the teacher. Football boots were always left on in class and mud from the cogs thrown at each other, behind the teacher's back. We had a very patient Head Master, Joe McHugh, and he would clap his hands and say, *"Christ, boys! I've children at home and they're not half as bad as ye fellas"*. He drove us to football trials and games in Sligo and round the county, and always called to his favourite *'watering hole'* on his way home

41

from our matches. I remember when he died. We carried his coffin, shoulder high to the graveyard from Easkey Church, for a distance of at least one and a half miles, to Roslea Cemetery. He was a brilliant Woodwork and Mechanical Drawing Teacher. He could be very annoyed if he thought a boy could progress better, but was not applying himself. Then, he would call other fellows, *'bloody clown'*, which was his favourite description of fourteen and fifteen year olds, who were acting giddy.

Jim McCabe was our Rural Science Teacher. He had won an 'All Ireland Medal' with Cavan in the Polo Grounds in 1948. When Jim left Easkey, he pursued further studies and progressed to a higher career. He eventually worked for the World Bank in New York. I was very happy to renew my acquaintance with him recently. I never thought he would remember me, but he did. And, he was really elated to think I called on my two crutches to see him. Margaret Kenny, now Mrs. Paddy Kilcullen, was our English and Irish Teacher, and was well able to control us. She took the *'wind out of my sails'* one day by saying to me, *"Has your mother anything better to do with her money than sending you to the 'Tech'?"*

Mrs. Duffy, taught us Business Methods, but, alas, we boys thought it was a *'girl's subject'*, and the affable Colm Mularkey of Tubbercurry was our Mechanical and Woodwork Teacher. He had won a 'Home Junior - All Ireland' football medal with Sligo in 1953, and was another hero of ours. Rural Science was a great favourite with the boys, as was plant and insect collections. We would survey fields and we would map them from the logbook, and we could grow vegetables for marks in our 'Group-Cert', and, also, have a vegetable plot at home. Gerry Donagher, who was our Teacher, then, had just come to Easkey as a new young Teacher, and later became Headmaster. He is now retired.

We had to learn to grow trees, and each of us were given six sitka spruce saplings to bring home. I remember bringing them home on the back of my bicycle. Four of them are now forty feet high. The other two, I'm afraid, I cut them with the scythe, when cutting the grass round them when they were small. With three years of second level education, we were ready for the world. Some fellows became 'Gardaí' and others took Forestry and Agricultural Science jobs and Insurance Reps., etc. Fred Conlon became an Art Teacher and a world renowned Sculptor. Other fellows became

Electricians and Carpenters and eventually Building Contractors and more fellows became good Farmers. The girls in our class all excelled in many professions.

Fred Conlon 1943 – 2005

Fred's talent had already been spotted while we were still in school. We all knew there was something special about him from his paintings and artwork. But little could we have imagined that he would go on to such high achievements. Over the years, he despised the concept of celebrity and I was privileged to be with him a few nights before he died. May he rest in peace.

Before exam time, when it came to inspecting my garden, for our Rural Science exam, the Rural Science Teacher called to take a photograph. Everything was growing but so were the weeds. He said the weeds might not show up in the photograph and I *"might get away with it,"* which I did. Fr. McGuiness was our Spiritual Director, and he got us all to join the 'Pioneers'. I am happy to say I kept my pledge although two of my colleagues who kept it are now dead, (John Feeney, a Garda, just retired, and Padraic Kilcullen, an Electrical Contractor). I also managed to stay away from cigarettes, even though I'd tried one or two as a young fellow. They put a bad taste on my mouth. But, staying away from those vices did not keep me from M.S., as I will outline later.

Now, in the year 2006, my grandson Daragh is in infants class in Ballinleg School. The teachers and pupils are at the point of moving back to the school on completion of a major extension, a project costing €300,000 with state of the art facilities. The extension is due to be opened by Bishop Fleming on 7th December this year.

Boys from Easkey Vocational School 1957/58

Front Row; Matt Keaveney, Tommy Kelly, Jackie Conlon, Charlie Meehan, Mr McHugh & Mr Donagher (Teachers) Noel Keenan, Noel Kilcullen, Martin Gordon, Pauric McBain.

Middle Row; Vincent McHugh, Vincent Cuffe, Martin Murray, Francis Lyons, John Monds, Pat Kilcullen, Eamon Carney, John Kennedy, P.J. Conlon.

Back Row; Pee Connaughton, T.J. Lyons, Peter Brady, Pat O'Connell, Michael Maloney, Aidan Caffrey, Michael Dowd, Jimmy Feeney, Dermot Conlon, John Feeney.

8

The Arrival of Radio and Electricity

In 1946 I remember the excitement of the arrival of a totally new dimension to our house - the new PYE radio. The electrical man of our area, Jim Armstrong of Leekfield, arrived with it in a big cardboard box on the back of his bicycle. The installation of it was a major project.

Firstly, a tall ariel had to be erected on the chimney and a wire taken through the bottom sash of the kitchen window, beside where the radio was to be situated on a small table. An earth rod had to go in the ground as a lightening conductor. The wet battery which stood proudly at its left hand side, had to be hooked up to the dry battery in the radio. This was how it would be powered, as we had not got electricity at that stage. My father always dated the dry battery and monitored its durability. There had to be a spare wet battery kept charged and alternated with the one in use as it would need recharging every few weeks. The main problem with this was that the radio was liable to give up in the middle of an exciting football match, and so you had to be quick making the change over.

People were very sparing in their use of this new device and only turned it on for the news and ceile music on a Saturday night.

Then in 1955 Rural Electrification came to our parishes. This was a major project and all the available farmers and young men were employed. The work involved digging the holes with the spade, shovel and pick-axe. They were required to dig two and a half holes per day. The poles had to be 'snigged' (pulled along the ground by horse and rope) through the fields by a farmer, Richard Neary (RIP). To raise them involved a pair of light poles lashed together with a short rope. The wages they got was £5 8s 6d. I remember three men could raise a pole. Siting them in line was a skilled job. My age group was in National School but it left a major imprint on our minds.

Because of the fact that the electricity was so advanced compared to our way of life, we had to attend demonstrations, to be educated as it were, regarding the safe and efficient use of the appliances. The levy of ground rent on the enclosed floor area of our dwellings and sheds that had doors and windows was a major talking point.

The word spread that if you removed the doors off the sheds you avoided ground rent. One local man who had not heard of the loophole in the rule became very irate when the E.S.B. official began measuring his ass house and his hen house. He told them in no uncertain terms that his *"ass and hens wanted no light."* Another householder only got one light in the kitchen. The reason for no light points in the bedroom was that they would be sleeping there and required no light. Another person would not get the electricity installed because she had a thatched house and *"it might burn it".* Another wit said the woman *"would have to sweep the kitchen floor, as the more efficient light would show up the dust".* So much for the advent of what turned out to be one of the most essential commodities of the 20th century and beyond.

In 1961 the first black and white televisions appeared in our locality. Pat Sexton in the Jersey Bar had one in the kitchen and the crowds spilled out on to the yard outside as we all came to watch the All-Ireland Final between Down and Offaly.

Spreading the Light.

27/10/55.

There is great escitement in our Parish for the past few weeks. All the escitement is caused by the advent of the electricity. light.

There are poles and wires and E. S. B. men all over the place. In our house alone there is nothing talked about only, plugs, switches, and fuses. Some people say that we will have light for Christmas. Mammy says that it will be welcome anytime it comes. About two years ago E. S. B. men made a survey of our Parish. That time some

people did not sign on.
But (so) our Parish guild of
Muintir na Tire set to work
and we are high on the
Rural Electrification list. now
The
wiring of the Parish is
making rapid progress.
The holes for the poles are
over sixe feet deep but the
gangs of men that dig
them are fast workers and
dig them very quickly.
Other men have gadgets
attached to their boots for
climbing poles to fit wires
on the pylons.
We love
watching them work, and as I'm
sure that there isn't a boy
in our school that who hasn't

his pockets full with scraps
of wire that the men cut
off the coils.
Mammy says that there will
be no good got out of us
untill the E. S. B. men
leave. There will be
no good of the Mothers
either because they are
always talking about,
washers, driers, irons and lights.
Mammy says that no one
will get a clean shirt
unless she gets a washer.
                    There are
some very old fashioned
people in our Parish.
One old man named Seamus
Bray. who lives up near
the mountain said (that)
that the light in a bottle

will make people blind.
Another old fellow said that
an oil lamp was good enough
for his father and it good
enough for him too.

28/10/53 When they saw their
neighbours houses wired they
got their houses wired as well.
The old man that said the
lights in the bottle would make
people "blind" has ordered a
new "Moffat", cooker.
When the light was switched
on in the neighouring parish
one family left the light on
12/11/55. for two days. They were
afraid to touch the
switches and they were
tired blowing at the bulb.
                              I will
be delighted when the

Electrification come (beeaco)
because I will get a rest
from drawing in turf and
sticks. Mammy said
that she (wo) will make
nice things for tea.
✓ Electricity is a great blessing
Corrections.
Off, off, off, until, until
until.

Bynnina,
Dromard,
Co Sligo.
3/11/55.

To.
F. Harry and Son, Ltd.,
47 Fleet St.,
Dublin.
Dear Sir.
Will

Extract from my school copy entitled 'Spreading the Light'

9

My Construction Years

During my 'Tech' days, I was advised by my Woodwork Teacher, to pursue a Woodwork Teaching Course in Wexford. But I could not avail of it, because I lived with my widowed mother, and there was no sponsorship at that time. I remember my mother being 'over the moon', when a Council Official asked her if I would work for the summer holidays. The job consisted of drawing barrels of water with our ass and cart, and filling barrels to supply the tarmacadam machine and steamroller, as the County Council laid a tarmacadam surface on the coast road, along where I live. In previous summers they had completed sections as far as the Mill Corner near us. So, I got the job on the last section.

I had to keep a barrel full of water to fill the machinery, as it was the way to keep the tar from sticking to the rollers. I was fourteen years old and the bucket of water was still heavy to lift from water sources. I was paid £1 old money per day. Most of my wages was for the use of my donkey and cart. That was my first introduction to the work force, which I enjoyed at the time, even though I had to spend time in hospital to have two toenails removed because my wellingtons were belonging to my mother and too small for my growing feet, and my toes got infected. I also worked with Jimmy McMunn, my neighbour, re-roofing old thatched houses, a very unhealthy job and no facemasks were used at the time.

That was just after my 'Tech' days. Also, after my casual jobs, it was time to go into the workforce - fulltime. My mother kept praying to Saint Joseph, the patron of carpenters, that I would become one. I thought GWI, the new joinery works, was the place to go, to serve my time. Young fellows had to be hanging around the front gate as the boss, Jimmy Kiernan, was rushing in at eight o'clock each morning. The story was that, if a sharp young fellow caught his eye on his way in, he would shout and say, *"Get in and start"*. I did not see him the few days I waited around, but a young fellow called Tom McNulty, who was more persistent than I, got the start of his 'professional' life.

I was anxious to get going, and I met a builder - Jimmy McHugh, who was a brother of our Headmaster, Joe, in Easkey. To my joy, he gave me a job. The first job was the spade and shovel, and I was told to dig a hole for a septic tank in Beltra wood, as he was doing a renovation job on the local hall, which was the hub of entertainment in our parish. No doubt, the worn spade and the bad shovel and also all of the tree roots left my first hole very difficult to dig.

The J.C.B. wasn't introduced to Ireland in 1960, but, digging was the way to 'blood-in' a young fellow. Mixing concrete and mortar, properly, was also an important part of construction activities. Concrete mixers were only used on big jobs, and, anyway, were much too expensive for country jobs. However, I progressed to the hammer and handsaw, and plane and chisel. I could make sash windows, fit floors and ceilings, and hang doors. I could make sash windows with 'any of them'. Another schoolmate of mind got a job with Jimmy, also. Vincie McHugh, who was great fun, joined the team of three or four men.

With that job done and experience gained, and cycling to work, sometimes ten miles away, I gained confidence and got my neighbour, John White, to put in a word for me with a building contractor who was doing an amount of work in our area. Joseph (Josie) Scanlon & Brothers were to be my bosses for the next ten years. This was 'big stuff', as National Schools were the main projects. It was a wonderful experience and I ended up a good carpenter. Josie was a legendary Sligo footballer, who was captain of the only Sligo team to win an All Ireland Junior Championship in 1935, and was a hero to me.

All carpentry work, at the time, was done, solely, by hand tools. Cutting roofs was no bother to us – even with a blunt handsaw, sometimes. If I had a 'Diston', it was the Rolls Royce of saws, and 'a dream come true' for every carpenter to own an American 'Diston' handsaw. But, they became dull, also, and had to be turned upside down on the saw-horse to be re-sharpened with the 'three-corner file'. That was a skill in itself, as the rubs (slides) had to be right to get the saw sharpened properly. The wood plane was, also, kept in good 'nick' as were the chisels - all had to be sharpened on the hone. The screwdriver was the only way for screwing, with the bradawl to start the screw.

Of course, the small hand hatchet was used when shuttering for concrete beams and lintels, before 'precast' was heard tell of. We also cased for windowsills and dwarf walls for timber floors. We cased for ring beams, also. A lot of casing was done on houses. Concrete blocks were made in the sand pit, by hand machines. It was another sickening task. Also, we had to 'raise' sand and gravel, sometimes, and fill it onto small non-tipper trucks and tractor trailers. We sieved and washed the stand for plastering, in a water barrel, with an overflow three quarter way up on the barrel. The sand stayed in the barrel and the muck flowed away. Then, we would throw the barrel on its side and shovel out the clean sand. Machine tools were unheard of, and I remember buying my first 'Black and Decker' drill and saw attachments in the mid sixties. It was a major step forward. Then, an electric planer, but it was only 'middling' value, because the cutters were ordinary steel and blunted too quickly. Also, bench saws appeared (portable ones for the building sites and the skill-saw), which was the very best thing, ever.

Even safety was not a major concern, as most fellows still had their fingers attached, as our woodwork teacher, Colm Mularkey, told us when at school, *"keep your hands behind your work and you will never cut yourself"*. Then, the 'Kango' appeared (another major step forward). It replaced the lump hammer and 'cold chisel' when chasing for conduits, and also forming holes in walls. I know the first Kangos were big and clumsy, and sometimes cracked the walls, due to strong fellows working them. I could not attempt to write about all the modern equipment, even concrete blocks started to come on tipper lorries, and were tipped near the roadside, as sites were not prepared like nowadays. They had to be carried, one or two at a time, through the muck and up a makeshift wooden ladder, similar to what I saw a recently in Megjegorie. Then (the sixties), and now, in the twenty first century, totally different methods were used.

I remember a builder with his car and trailer, thought he was a big fellow, as he was building two bungalows beside each other. He was standing at the counter, beside me, in a builders' suppliers, telling the boy behind the counter to put it down to 'the scheme'. He was charging bits of material to his account.

I remember the first new bungalow my partner and myself built in 1967 at a cost of £4,850 old money, complete. I know Micheál Kearins won't mind me recalling this one, as it was his new house.

Just before my years in construction, a builder told a man that it would cost £80 old money, extra, to have a bathroom in his house. The man told him that it was, *"All right"*, and that *"the cow byre was good enough as a toilet, as it was good enough for his forefathers"* and now for him. That was the era when spring water was too far away, to pump it into the dwelling houses.

Mains water was not even contemplated in rural areas. Another way was to build an underground storage tank at the rear of the new house and have a hand pump fitted to the back wall, and pump it up to the storage tank in the attic space. Gravity took care of the rest. Then, the min-electric pump came along and many of them were fitted in the hot press or under the bath, whichever was the shortest way. Still, everybody went to the spring well for a bucket full, for making tea. Also, pre the bathroom, the 'slop bucket' and the 'chamber pot' were the normal, to have as room service. All the above were not too hygienic, but still, this was the way it was, in the early span of my lifetime. This is life as I saw it, 'till the growth of the eighties.

During my working life, it was prudent to accumulate as many building sites as possible, as a nest egg, and hence, build up a portfolio. Naturally, that was my way, as well as others, in the seventies and eighties. But, alas, in the late eighties, as speculation was getting rife, my health started to deteriorate. And consequently, my concentration in life, started to decline, and I had to sell some of my property. Missed opportunities were often part of my life.

Even though, I was fortunate enough to be able to buy nine acres in 1972 for £1,600.00 decimal currency, which was less than £200.00 an acre. And, incidentally, a neighbour told me I was *"mad in the head"* to buy it. Surely, they were unrestricted times in my young days. Sites could be bought for a couple of hundred pounds, and no bother to get planning permission. The big problem was the bank Manager (at least the one I dealt with). I asked him could I get a loan of £5,000, to buy a farm near Sligo town. He looked at me over his glasses and said, *"How would you pay it back?"* I said, *"Sure! I can sell a few sites off it and free the cost"*. *"That's no way"*, he scoffed. I thought I was still at school, and he was a teacher.

The same occurrence happened at least twice with other available, reasonable properties. Young fellows were much easier put off at the time. Even though some of my counterparts were not, and they are millionaires today. I made various attempts to get on the larger property ladder, but for some reason, I had obstacles of one kind or another. One time, in 1975, I had a nice, small field in my sights, and was hoping to buy it, when I got sick. The Auctioneer got a higher bid, but I was on my back in Merlin Park Hospital, in Galway, with Sarcoidosis. Even though he wrote to me, (incidentally, there was no mobile phones at that time), I was too sick to pursue the deal.

Another time, I had an opportunity to get going on a housing estate. The Auctioneer rang me and told me that he was selling sites on what turned out to be one of the biggest housing estates in my town. He told me that each site, for a pair of semidetached houses, would cost £2,000, and we would have to pay nothing, until we built and sold the houses. At that time, 'build and sell' was the way builders were starting to operate, and then they could buy more sites, and it was a great opportunity to get started. But, unfortunately, for various reasons this deal didn't work out for me.

The point I make by writing this is that, young people should follow their dreams if at all feasible. That was it for years, except build, build, build. Between £3,500.00 and £6,000.00 was the cost of leaving a house finished and ready to live in. Naturally, the standard of construction was basic, as I have stated already – no cavity wall insulation, no double-glazed windows, no PVC facia, soffits, doors or windows. Gun barrel piping was used in all central heating systems, and chipboard floors in all bedrooms, and often in the bathroom, as well. White sanitary-ware was used, with an extra £50.00 charge for a coloured suite. No fitted kitchens or wardrobes were made, that time. Roof tiles were all the go, except, if you were really rich, you could afford to buy slates. Tarmacadam was very expensive, with gravel drive ways being the normal, with the only exception being a garage at the side of the house, if you had a car. It was important to keep it in the garage at night, especially if you lived near the sea. Like the gun barrel piping, the cars used to rust in a few years.

All I have mentioned, both house and car materials were not meant to last more than a few years. But at the time, people were gullible and knew no better and it was money down the drain, unwittingly. Most of the houses built in the sixties and seventies were rebuilt, or are totally remodelled, by now. Landscaping was unheard of at the time. One thing was for certain – that there was a sacred heart light under the picture of the Sacred Heart in the living room, which has fast disappeared from that time. I remember the first woman that I advised to invest in a fitted kitchen, she replied, *"What would that cost me?"* I told her the price and she said that she would *"rather send the money to the famine areas of the world"*.

Still, good humour and 'great wit' played a huge part between all construction workers. I worked with the very best of men. A lot of them went forward to be very successful, today. And, as I talked to another retired construction worker, he said to me, recently, *"you have not enjoyed life, unless you worked on a building site in the sixties and seventies"*.

Near-misses (accidents) were abundant in these years, and I recall a few of them. Once, in 1975, an American cousin (called Tom Carney), called to see me on a building site. The first thing he told me was that he was a safety inspector on building sites in Connecticut. Then he told me, that if he inspected us, Irish builders, he would have us all closed down and fined, heavily. Also, he said, *"Your men should be wearing hard hats"* and I simply said back to him, *"Ah! Sure, nothing ever goes wrong around here"*. With that, our labourer, Bertie, came to the doorway, with the blood dripping from his chin. What had happened was, that a carpenter was working on the roof timber, had let his hammer fall and it hit Bertie on the head. *"Now!"* said the 'Yank', *"What did I tell you?"* What could I say? Anyway, Bertie had to be taken to Nurse Allen, in Ballisadare, and plastered up.

Another day, when Bertie was climbing the ladder, I saw flames coming from his trousers. It was time to throw a bucket of water at him. Apparently, he was burning cement bags, and had kicked them together. A spark caught in the fold of his trousers. The plasterer whom he was attending, Liam Murray, said he *"Should not have been wearing his Sunday trousers, anyway"*.

Another near fatality, on a job, in my young days, happened at a roofing job on Creevalea Church, near Dromahair. The man working at the roof timber, beside me, Tommy Scanlon, fell from the apex, straight down onto the floor, where the Altar site was. He only had a broken ankle. One of the witty boys on the job said that, *"only for he fell where the altar site was, he would be killed"*. The tail-end of the story was that, panic set in and a man jumped into the bosses' car, to go to Dromahair, to get the doctor. But, he lost control of it, at a bridge, and crashed and wrote-off the car and hurt himself. I met a former work colleague, recently in hospital, Mick McGuinn, from Coolaney, and we went over the incident. And, also, over the time when a ton of highly stacked cement toppled over on Mick, and ruptured him.

Over the years, I have been fortunate, to meet and interact with a good number of the construction people, in the northwest - from the simple and sometimes self-taught fellows of my time, to the highly educated and totally competent workforce of today, who are totally abreast of the current boom in construction. It is great to see the transformation in my lifetime, as regards the Irish construction industry. I recall some competent builders like, Felix McHugh, Martin Wilson, Sean Kilgannon, Tommy Horan, Sean McGuire, Ivan Hamilton, Leslie Hamilton, Paddy Healy, Paddy Egan, Donal Kelly, Liam Scott, Hugh Kilgallen, P J Reynolds, Tom Currid, Peter & Martin Savage. All those men, I have good memories of - either they worked for me, through time, or I worked for them at stonework, in my later years. I was proudly associated with each and every man. In the past few years, the FÁS Training Authority are training apprentices to the highest standard. They are a credit to themselves, their instructors and their families. I pay tribute to each and every one of them.

My son Paul with Aidan Hegarty and myself at tea-break on site

9

Debbie in 1961

'Debbie' was the name given by the Meteorologists to the largest windstorm that my generation has ever witnessed. It occurred in September 1961, on Saturday the 16th, at eleven o'clock in the morning. By midday, it was at its fiercest. At the time, I was working for Josie Scanlon Builders, and we were working on a new bungalow in the locality for Michael Dowdican, who lived two miles from my home in Bunnina. Incidentally, the house cost £1,800, and for that money, included a bathroom and four good-sized bedrooms.

At the time, a carpenter's job was to make the hot press, wardrobes and kitchen presses. I was making the hot press on the day of the big storm, when I saw Michael going out to his field. He was wearing only a shirt and trousers, and went to unruffle the hand-shakings, which the big wind was beginning to toss. The next thing I saw was the hay, just taking off, and he was left with his arms on the one he was fixing. Some of the hay got stuck in the hedge, but most of it went out of sight altogether. As one o'clock was approaching, it was time for me to finish work, as we did every Saturday, to go home on my bicycle. This was a treacherous journey if there was ever one, as trees and telephone wires were knocked down and thrown across the road. Galvanized roofs and slates were blown off a lot of houses. With the luck of God, I made it home intact to a fine dinner cooked by my mother. Although we had electricity installed, she did not depend on it. She still cooked on the open fire. As they say, *"old habits die hard"*, but, the old ways proved the best, on that occasion of turmoil.

On Monday morning, it was work as usual, but I'm afraid, Josie Scanlon did not get a lot of value out of us workers that day, when he needed us most to be in top working form, due to all the storm damage on the job and all over the country. I was working with the greatest comedians around, who would put the likes of 'Brendan Grace' to shame. The plasterers, Jim Durkin and Seamus Mannion, were from Strandhill and were always going on about that weekend, no doubt, with a little exaggeration, to spice it up.

One tale was retold many times after 'Debbie', and that was about all the galvanized roofs, hay and grain crops that were blown across to their shore and were all held on the sandbanks in Strandhill. The local Strandhill people were lucky, and were able to re-roof their sheds, and trash our grain with all of our materials. In reply, I answered that, 'it was an ill wind that didn't blow somebody good'. Jim used to say that I came *"from the 'blue-grass country'"* and that *"if a farmer mislaid his stick, in our fields in the morning, he would not be able to find it in the evening, because the grass would have grown so much for the day"*. This type of jibing would continue through the working day, one trying to outdo the other. The memory of the destruction left in the aftermath of 'Debbie' is still fresh in my generation's memories, and allows us to understand the world calamities that we hear about today.

My mother (Mary Ellen Maye) on her final return from New York, taken on board the Cunard Liner, 'Sky', on 26th June 1935

My Carney ancestoral home in Croch Móre, Dromard

The Carney resting place in Dromard Cemetry (including Tommy Carney's dog 'Jess')

10

Bestra Hall

Amateur drama was always an important part of rural life in Dromard, in the sixties. Naturally, every young boy and girl, aspired to 'playing their part' in society, and what better way to exercise young brains, and have fun at the same time, than to be part of the Advent play. The pastime, for the long winter nights, was important, as Advent was the churches' period for abstinence, before the Christmas festivities.

Drama performances were a useful way of raising money for the football club, or what ever needed extra cash to survive, in the parish. Beltra Hall was a much used venue for the Drama Society, which, for the previous generations, was the 'Mecca', for drama and dancing. They also produced three act plays with good story lines. They were simple and hilarious and good fun. It attracted me, and I enjoyed smaller parts, as young people had to be 'blooded' into acting. One of the plays was, 'The Green Boxeen'. 'Queer Times' was another one.

Then, we felt it was a good idea to raise money for our Saint Patrick's Football Club. So, we started about producing a three act play called, 'A Bolt From The Blue', in Dan O'Connor's hall in Skreen. But, alas, we thought it would all work out good on the night it was being staged, but not enough attention was paid to learning our lines. Our local Curate, Father Gallagher, was also our Director, and was a bit lenient on us as we played indoor football between all the girls and boys, on mixed teams, instead of learning our lines or how to act, properly. It was much more fun than learning boring parts for the night of the play.

In the play was, Pauline Kennedy, Antoinette Cummins, Annie Kilgallen, Madeline Kilgallen, Noreen Mahon, Antoinette Mahon, Sean Nealon, Shamie Donegan, Frank Leonard, Michael Kennedy and myself. As a strange coincidence, Pauline's part was as a daughter of mine. She had caught my eye, in much earlier times, in Dan's hall, when she used to be helping her mother and Skreen ICA with teas and snacks at the ICA dances. This play is how romance started for us.

I sometimes left her home on the bar of my bicycle – until her mother wanted to know how she got the grease on her lovely fawn coat. That time, we had our bicycles well oiled, and 'it' was from the pinion joint, where the handlebars go through the frame. This is what caused the black stain on Pauline's coat. After that, our friend, Padraic McMunn, used to leave the girls

66

home, in his father's 'Austin' van. On the night of our performance of 'A Bolt From The Blue', it was *'iffy'* enough, but it still filled Dan's hall with patrons. But, two fellows started a fight at the rear of the crowd, and to our horror, everyone stood up and looked around at them, thinking it was all part of the entertainment. Amateur drama was surely living up to its name at the time.

Now, I'm married to Pauline, the greatest wife a man could have. After thirty-seven years, I've got the chance to announce it!

Beltra Show, which takes place at the end of each summer, has been part of life in our parish for the past ninety-five years. I have been a member all my life, as was my father and mother before me. It has always been a great social occasion and draws crowds from far and near. I look forward to it every year and its keen competition in such a broad range of catagories never ceases to amaze me.

96th Beltra Show Committee on Show Day 2006
Standing from left; Ann Campbell, Ann James, Beatrice Dowd, Edel Kearins (Secretary), Ann Kearins, Philis McDonagh, Thomàs James, Hughie James, Frances Murray, Pat Rush, Martin Wilson (Chairman).
Front Row Left to right; David James, Mary James, Molly Rush, Corlie Campbell (President R.I.P.), Eamon Carney.

Beltra Hall

Beltra Hall & Show Committee on the occasion of the
60th Wedding Anniversary of Pat & Molly Rush
Seated from left to right; Aleck Crichton, Eamon Carney, Pat & Molly Rush, Joan
Crichton (R.I.P.), Martin Wilson (Chairman) Alister Kee
Standing; Audrey Kee (Secretary), Lorraine Wilson, Beatrice Dowd, Dessie Brady, Mary
Agnes Maye, Hughie & Mary James, John Connolly, Nora McHugh, Christina Brady,
Marie McMunn, Noel Sexton, Mary McCarthy, Eileen McDonagh,
Paddy & Barbara Rolston.

11

My GAA Life 1959 to 1990

I preface my GAA life with my childhood memories from the fifties. Gaelic football was always central to my life, but it was difficult to come to terms with the fact that Micheál Kearins could play and score much better than any of us in National School. It was great to be playing with him because when we played we won, every time. School tournaments in the west Sligo area in the mid fifties, were all the go - and we won our share of them! Before Board Na Nóg, that was the way to our football skills.

As we grew older, it became clear that we were playing with the most exceptionally talented 'forward' the country had ever seen. No doubt, our Saint Patrick's GAA Club, of which I am now President, is very proud of his footballing stardom, which contributed to us fellows winning the Senior Championship on five occasions, and Senior League on seven occasions in the sixties and seventies and eighties.

I'll never forget the large crowds of passionate supporters always swelling the sidelines eagerly shouting and cheering and sometimes resorting to 'fisticuffs' and brawls, all of which is alien to modern times. I am still conscious of the marvellous physique and ability of the young men of that footballing era.

I remember in my young life during the 1950/60's when mentors of teams were very cunning and always tried to have their team at their strongest – but the G.A.A. rule book was not always adhered to. This was one reason that Parish team photographs were not allowed. Sometimes the team was 'top heavy' with a few stars from elsewhere.

If this was discovered to be the case by the opposition it necessitated an objection to the county board, with all the evidence possible and maybe illegal evidence to justify the players proper inclusion in that team.

For the objection to be valid it had to be written on Irish-made note paper i.e., when held up to light everybody had to be able to see the 'watermark'. Also, the objection had to have an 'Irish pound note' pinned to it.

If any of those two above that I mentioned were not valid the objection was ruled out of order straight away. Another way to justify that a player was legal, was if he had a relative in the parish and it could be claimed the footballer worked and lived part time with them. In the fifties and sixties and before, mentors felt it a great achievement to 'get away with it' especially if it was a final.

My early football memories after our national school days were of cycling to the opening of the Markievicz Park soon after my father's death in 1955. Prior to Markievicz Park, I remember seeing games on the Circular Road field, the home of Craobh Rua, where the famous, Peter Laffey of Mayo football fame, used to graze his cow. It was owned by Jerry Mannion, father of Dermot Mannion CEO Air Lingus. I also recall that Markievicz Park had no dressing rooms in the early days. County teams togged out in the Café Cario, in the town, and arrived by car or van for the game.

At that period in the 1950's -60's, some of us young fellows were attracted to watching Sligo Rovers playing soccer but this was illegal as the GAA rule book ruled it out. There was a 'Vigilance Committee' who spied on young fellows who went to The Showgrounds. We used to wear dark glasses and a hat and scarf in order to get away with it. I remember their star players' - Johnnie Armstrong was a Flyer on the Left Wing and they had a foreign fellow called Straka. The two other stars we came to admire were David Pugh and Gerry Mitchell who later played with our Sligo GAA team.

Imagine, Sligo was the county who, in 1971, called for and got, the removal of the 'foreign games ban' from the rule book. Rivalry was very, rife at that time, and footballers were 'traitors' for playing soccer, as it was known as a foreign game. We even played a bit of soccer, and I could easily say, Micheál Kearins could be the present day Roy Keane. How and ever, Gaelic football was our number one sport, and we were fortunate enough to have the best days of our lives, through our involvement in it, both playing, and myself later, in administration.

My very first memory of GAA activity in Skreen was of me being brought on the team bus to the County Junior Final in 1952, between Skreen and Keash in Ballymote. That time the club had to hire a CIE large bus to bring the team and supporters to the final. My mother and Marcella Duffy, the new teacher, were with me. I remember that it was a brilliant occasion, especially to experience the big strong fit young men, matched to a Keash team of equal structure. My other memories of GAA activity, which was every Sunday, was when my Father cycled with me on a large tricycle to our local sports field, known as Eddie McMunn's Field.

Even though this was long before teams amalgatmated, there was enough young men and women from Dromard to have their own Football, Hurling and Camoige teams. There was huge rivalry between parishes at the time. I saw many a violent row; I even saw a man breaking his leg in a game. Most teams at the time always had their Rowdies who were noted and always challenged by the opposition. As a child, it was very frightening to see so much blood and so many black eyes. I know now that that was 1950's way of showing pride and passion.

After all games everybody retired to the local pubs. I exclude all comments from the girls camogie team who played their games in a smaller field of Sweeney's well away from any of the pubs. I still recall the ladies who played and I still enjoy chats about it with Vera Rushe and Maura Bradley.

My club experience was similar as no rural club had the luxury of dressing rooms or shower facilities. But, we were lucky in that respect, as we had to cross a stream to get to out pitch ('*Dan's Field*'), and we could wash the muck and cow dung off ourselves just before we went to the hedge where we had our clothes, sometimes pushed well up on a bush. It often happened that the cattle chewed the sleeves of shirts and trousers, which was a '*sickener*' especially if we happened to be on our way to a dance or a social engagement.

That was the way all footballers enjoyed their leisure evenings and played until it got dark and sometimes even wet and gloomy. This prevailed until St.Patrick's club acquired and developed its own facilities in 1984.

At the moment, my club, Saint Patrick's, is in transition to a new structure, where we have a very competent Board Na Nóg, and a very enthusiastic team of boys and girls and I am looking forward to seeing them doing the club proud, once again. Life has gone the full circle for me, from total involvement in GAA affairs in the club, the County Board, then the Connaught Council, and at a time when I would like to have progressed to Central Council, I got MS. So, between my working life, social involvement of all sorts, and GAA affairs, my time at home was quite short. My good wife, Pauline, almost single-handedly, reared our six children, even though she gives me credit for helping with the bathing on Saturday nights, and with 'hoovering' on Sunday mornings.

My first serious introduction to competitive football was in Ballymote, in 1960, where we contested the County Minor Final against Ballymote. Our mentors thought that we were going to be beaten on the day, and introduced a large young fellow as a replacement. I can still see Seamus Leonard (a big frame of a fellow) running onto the pitch. Even at twenty one, everybody knew it was obvious, he was over age. Anyway, the game ended in a draw, and sure enough, the Ballymote mentors doubted our team make up, and objected to the County Board. They also discovered that we had four ineligible players, who were from the Dromore West and Templeboy clubs, as was normal for clubs at the time, as there was no photographs allowed and, no team selector wanted the illegal players to be noticed. They were also put on the team sheet under a young fellows name from the parish. That particular objection to us, took a lot of time on our case, and most of us had to go to the County Board meeting in Collooney Courthouse. I'll never forget it.

It was a typical court scene, with Tom Kilcoyne, County Secretary, and the Chairman, Peter Laffey, on the front bench, and various top officials behind them. At the end of the meeting, we were proved illegal, so the Minor Championship was awarded to Ballymote. We were totally disillusioned, and Mícheál Kearins said he *"would never be seen at a meeting again."* I did not seem convinced, and it became clearer to us, that the 'Rule Book' was the only way to achieve progress. As if to prove this, it was on the playing pitch that Mícheál achieved progress on our behalf, on his way to stardom, (and also, our club, Saint Patrick's).

I enjoyed being their 'Gaffer' as Eugene McGee, journalist, calls the committed club all-rounder. Having said that, we had an outstanding committed panel, who did not drink alcohol, and two of them, who did, used to go off it for the football season.

I remember Mícheál Kearins travelling to America in 1967, with the Connaught Team, on a tour. The first thing he told me when he came home was that he broke his 'pledge'. I thought it was the worst thing he ever told me. I thought this would mean other fellows on the team, including myself, would break our pledge and that our football form would suffer. Still, in 1988 and 1989, we won the Sligo Senior Championship, with *"a fairly advanced team"*, as was said at the time. (Even though Kearins and a few more had retired, it was a very proud occasion for me, as I was Vice Chairman of Sligo County Board, and Chairman of Activities. Also, I had progressed from Sligo County Board to represent them on the Connaught Council. It meant a lot to me to have Saint Patrick's representing Sligo in the Club Championship on two occasions, even though with no further progression.)

Another of my great friends who died in the eighties was Joe Masterson of Tubbercurry. He had the greatest wit and humour and was the greatest GAA man. The day of his funeral was the first time I discovered I could not walk in a Guard of Honour behind his coffin. Soon after that in 1989, I was diagnosed with MS. May Joe rest in peace. In tribute to Joe and Sligo's all time great forward, Micheal Kearins I want to quote now from Joe's piece in the GAA magazine of 1984;

IMPRESSIONS OF KEARINS

All sports have their outstanding exponents — all counties in GAA have their heroes — there is also the comparison between County and National status in the ratings in GAA. But in my opinion Mickey Kearins was the greatest wing-forward I have ever seen play in forty years of attending Gaelic games. Now and again the arguments range over the respective abilities of Giants in the various sports and I would never take part in such discussions unless 'like versus like' was the basis of the argument.

Some people insist on comparison of players over the one hundred years since the inception of the GAA. Others will be heard listing the attributes of a towering defender against the talents of a quicksilver forward — and the only result in those cases is an 'impasse'.

When knowledgeable people speak of the era just completed — Mickey Kearins will rate as the No. 1 Wing-Forward in general play and as a bonus the most accurate place kicker of his generation. The simplicity of his style and the effortless execution of every basic Gaelic football skill, left one awe struck and undoubtedly he would figure on 'The Greatest ever Gaelic football team' of his time.

In April 1981 Sligo Co. Board GAA paid tribute to Michael Kearins at the Sligo Park Hotel for his outstanding services to the County - It was in the form of a 'This is Your Life' in GAA style of programme. Devised and produced by Joe Masterson with a selected committee of GAA officials. The event was an outstanding success with over 300 people present to wine and dine as the 'Kearins Saga' was unfolded and the 'Greats of Ireland' paid him his last reward for the many hours of pleasure he had given to all GAA followers. He was presented with a beautifully inscribed piece of Innisfree Crystal and two stylistically designed framed pictures listing his attributes and achievements. "Sligo County Board and Joe Mastersons committee are to be congratulated on honouring Sligo's greatest forward — Mickey Kearins. Having watched Gaelic football for the Past thirty five years and having been privileged to play with and against many outstanding footballers in that time I have not seen a more accomplished kicker of the ball than Mickey Kearins.

We in Sligo have been fortunate in the fact that we have witnessed vintage Kearins performances at club and county level. Had the transfer fee been in operation in GAA — Mickey would probably be the first "Six million dollar man" — and this figure may be on the conservative side!! It was an honour to be asked to write about this great footballer and a pleasure also as one can always bask in the reflected glory even if one is not always centre stage.

MICKEY KEARINS – THE STATISTICAL SIDE

All Ireland Charts	No. 1 - 1966, 1968, 1972, 1973
Four Times No. 1	Totals – 3.90, 2.135, 4.130, 2.118
Connacht	No. 1 - 1972 Total 4.130
Records in All-Ireland charts	No. 2 - 1968 Total 2.135
Sligo Charts	Top Scorer 1962 to 1975
Century Club	Total 100 points = goals and points combined. Mickey Kearins was a member of this club for six years - a record in his time.

Over all: Mickey Kearins scored 36 goals and 1,158 points (1,266 points) in 215 games, League, Championship, Railway Cup, Tournaments and challenge games,

Club	2 Junior Championships
	2 Senior Championships (amalgamated)
	5 Senior Championships
	4 Senior Leagues
County	1 Connacht Championship
Railway Cup	2 Championships
All-Star Awards	One
Numerous Awards	Numerous trophies for tournaments etc
Connacht appearances	Thirteen

We were the last Sligo club to win the original 'Owen 'B' Hunt Cup' and the first club to be presented with the new one, in '88 and '89, respectively. The Saint Patrick's Captain on both occasions was my good neighbour, Seamus Reilly.

In the earlier years, in 1968, we had four talented minors on the County Minor Team, whom I was proud to have under my attention when Sligo reached the Minor All Ireland Final, only to be beaten by Cork, by one point. (This, I hope, will be taken a step further, in my lifetime, when some Sligo team will win at all Ireland level). The four Saint Patrick's football stars, in 1968 where, John Kilgallon, Richie Boland, Peadar Kearins and Jimmy Kilgallon.

I remember going to collect Jimmy Kilgallon, my fellow club man, on the morning of the final, and his good mother, Mary, threw the 'tongs' after us, as we left her house. This was 'pistrogues' to send us luck, and it nearly worked as we were only one point behind at fulltime, bringing heartbreak on that day and since. This piece about the 'tongs' was recalled to me by Jimmy one evening, recently.

He also reminded me of many years ago, when he was closely involved in our club (maybe, more so than myself), he was going to the GAA North Divisional Board meeting, with the Chairman of the club, Patrick Kearins R.I.P. As they waited for the man with the car, (who never came) they decided to ask a neighbour, Jim Battle, to bring them. *"No bother!"* said Jim, *"Wait until I back my 'Mini' out of the turf shed"*. But, alas, Jim did not realize that the passenger door of his car was open, and, when he reversed out of the shed, he caught the door in the pillar and buckled it around the wrong way. No doubt, the boys could not go very far to the meeting that way. They told Jim to bring them over to myself (Eamon Carney), and that I would bring them, which I did. That was the start of me and my 'Morris Minor' going to all the GAA meetings in the North Divisional Board, for the next ten years.

I certainly liked what I saw, and I can honestly say that each and every GAA person that I had occasion to work with, both club, Divisional Boards (North and West), the Connaught Council, Sligo County Board, were all exemplary people. So, between 1960 and 2000, when I had to leave it all behind me, I enjoyed forty years of service to the most exemplary, voluntary and rewarding organization in Ireland.

The tradition and the will to emulate our seniors, always played a major role through the generations. Even through my young life, I was fortunate to interact with the most knowledgeable of men, none more so than Matt Brady, who was a former National School teacher of repute. Even in his retirement years, I enjoyed his archaic lifestyle, republicanism and his love of Gaelic games. I was proud to nominate Matt as Patron of Sligo County Board in 1970. He always gave his address to the Annual Convention in the Irish language and the words he used to me were, "By Jove! I will never speak a word of English to them". That was him, referring to the culture of our GAA people, to use Irish as much as possible.

Now, as President of Saint Patrick's, I will re-familiarize myself with pride of a piece of script written by Matt in our GAA magazine of 1984. He was training to be a National School Teacher in Dublin, and was in Croke Park on Bloody Sunday on November 21st 1920, a day he recounted in the St. Patrick's booklet of 1984, and this is his story:

"And this is the part of my narrative which I had intended to relate because it was during this period of my youth occurred the most dangerous and exciting day of my life. The day known since as 'Bloody Sunday', The IRA of this period and the British were locked in deadly conflict in Dublin and in many other places all over the country. A few months after our arrival there the struggle seemed to intensify and you could deem yourself lucky if you went into the city and arrived back without witnessing one of those street ambushes which made us so much afraid. And many of the most noteworthy of these fights took place within a few hundred yards of our institution on the North side.

I remember in particular one morning the Dean came in to the study Hall and gave us details of the happenings of the night before. "We had almost planned to wake you all up at midnight" he said "and give you a general absolution because the grounds were full of armed men". On that night one of our teachers was shot dead by the British in a raid on Fernside, his home a few hundred yards from St. Patrick's.

But again I am afraid the old master at Ross would chide me for straying from my original intention, I am trying to take those episodes in order and of course 'Bloody Sunday' was just around the corner. At that time we had a good football team in St Patrick's. The name of the team was 'Erin's Hope' and on the morning of 'Bloody Sunday' they had met the

Dun Laoghaire Commercials in the final of the Dublin Intermediate Championship, but I remember we were beaten.

When the students assembled in the hallway after dinner, like most defeated teams they decided to go down to the Park again to the big match between Dublin and Tipperary, two of the leading teams in the country at the time when they might perhaps witness the defeat of Dublin. And so it happened that at about three o'clock that evening a group of us gathered on the shilling side just outside the wire midway under where the Cusack Stand now stands. A few of them were from the Clonmel area of Tipperary and they were pointing out to us the Tipperary players. Tobin of Grangemockler, Shelly of Clonmel, Nea Shea of Fethard and of course we knew the McDonnells, Norris the Synotts of Dublin. But in a moment the game was on and what a game it was going to be according to appearances. I remember Tobin with the golden hair at midfield for Tipperary. He was very prominent.

Again the scene changed. An aeroplane flew low over the pitch and after a few slow circuits headed off again- I seem to remember over the Ballybough section and towards Malahide. Nobody gave it a second thought as planes were around every day. In a very short space of time the Black and Tans arrived in Crossley tenders on the Canal Bridge just outside the pitch and with a minimum of delay opened fire on the crowds in the field. The word passed round rapidly "They are firing."

From that moment nobody needed to be told 'Hurry'. There is no greater incentive to do so, than forty or fifty rifles crackling in you direction. Between where we stood and the boundary wall was only a distance of eight to ten yards and on all fours, the entire crowd headed for this wall, scaled it and dropped into Belvedere Rugby Football grounds. Across that field thousands of us (I think there were 15,000 at the match) raced head long to safety. At the lower end of the field we scaled another high wall and found ourselves outside an Artisan's cottage in Ballybough. We failed to gain admission to the living quarters but we got into a barn where the family stored potatoes and turf.

And now at the risk of being accused of a slight profanity, I must relate an incident which happened in that barn. One of our students, a Monaghan boy, sat on a pile of turf just opposite me. Most of us prayed. I myself promised God I'd never again stand in Croke Park, if I came safe. A promise I kept for a fortnight, but the Monaghan boy thought of the efficacy of the Act of Contrition, which he proceeded to say out loud. And this is how he said it;

"Oh my God I am heartily sorry for having offended Thee, and I detest my sins above every other evil because they displease Thee, my God." Here he left the text completely and added "the curse o'Hell on them." He never finished the Act of Contrition - even his own version of it.
In a few short years he stood before a class and maybe at some time he had the task of preparing them for Confession. I wonder if he remembered 'Bloody Sunday' when he himself said it. But of course times had changed and I feel certain he omitted the malediction he invoked on the Black and Tans that Sunday in the middle of the act he said in the barn at Ballybough".

Then I listen to my former great colleagues, Peter Laffey, Joe McMorrow, Brendan McAuley, Paddy Clifford, Padraic Gorman, John Higgins, John Leydon, Joe Queenan, and also Mickey Regan (of Keash), and Joe Masterson (of Tubbercurry) to name only a few, as they debated very serious and humorous issues. Now I am very happy to see men like, John Murphy and Tommy Kilcoyne, (who served as secretary all through my tme and since) enter the new era.

MEMBERS OF SLIGO COUNTY BOARD - 1984

Front Row (L-R) Luke Kilcoyne, Eamonn Carney, John Benson, John Higgins (Chairman), Michael F. Regan, Walter Kivlehan, Michael Donnellan, Michael Gannon, and Sean McGolderick (Sligo Champion Reporter of the day)
Middle Row (L-R) Sean Kilgallon, John Lee, Roger Eames, Michael Gallagher, Seamus Cummins, Frank Pugh, John Watters, Brendan Wynne, Peter Cooney, T.J.Murphy.
Back Row (L-R) Paddy Kearns, Michael McDonagh, Gerry Conway, Padraic Duffy, Tom Haran, James McDonagh, Neil Farry.

ST. PATRICK'S FOOTBALL TEAM IN THE EARLY '60'S

Front Row; Shamie Donegan (RIP), Andy Boland, Michael Cummins, Michéal Kearins (Capt.), Padraic Kilcullen (RIP), Edward Rush, Eamon Carney, Padraic McMunn, Vincie McHugh.
Back Row; Joe Cuffe, Frank Leonard, John Leonard (RIP), Padraic Cummins (RIP), Marty Kerrigan (RIP), Stanley Beckett, Kieran Corcoran and Jimmy Kilcullen (Mgr.)(RIP)

ST. PATRICK'S TEAM 21-YEAR REUNION
OF OUR FIRST SENIOR CHAMPIONSHIP IN 1968

Front Row; Eamon Carney, Patrick Kearins (RIP), Johnny Kiely, Michéal Kearins, Shamie Donegan (RIP), Brendan Kilcullen, Tommy Carroll (Chairman Sligo County Board), Padraic Kilcullen (RIP)
Middle Row; Paddy Joe Kilcullen, Joe Cuffe, Jimmy Kilcullen (RIP), Donal O'Connor, John Kilgallen, Jimmy Kilgallon, Paul Clarke, Edward Rush, Vincie McHugh.
Back Row; Thomas Cummins, Frank Leonard, Tom McMunn (RIP), Peadar Kearins, Stanley Beckett, Andy Boland, Padraic Cummins (RIP), Padraic McMunn, Tony Leonard.

Mícheál Ó Muircheartaigh, Patsy Cummins, Eamon Carney and Thomas Cummins
(Mayor of Sligo) with the Sam Maguire Cup on the occasion of the visit to Sligo by John
McKeever (Tyrone Player) to celebrate Tyrone's All Ireland win of 2004

Three of the best St. Patrick's mentors
Patricik Kearins, Jimmy Kilcullen and Tom Doudican

CONNACHT GAA COUNCIL 1985

Front row; Paddy Basquille (Mayo), M J 'Inky' Flaherty (RIP) (Galway), Frank Kenny (Roscommon), Dr. Donal Keenan (RIP) (Roscommon), George O'Toole (Leitrim), Johnny Mulvey (Mayo).

Back Row; Christy Loftus (Mayo), Christy Gallogly (RIP) (Leitrim), John O'Mahoney (Mayo), Eamon Carney (Sligo), Paddy Kearns (Sligo), Eamon Campion (Roscommon), Eamonn Tubman (Leitrim), Miko Kelly (Galway), Pa Burke (RIP) (Galway), Padraig Brennan (Roscommon).

Sligo was one of the two counties to vote against the removal of the controversial 'Rule 27' Ban in 1971. Despite this fact I'm especially pleased that Sligo proposed the motion at Congress 2005 to temporarily remove Rule 42 and allow the opening up of Croke Park to other sports, (simply on a 'good neighbour' basis) while they get their own stadiums to the level of Croke Park, both for rugby and soccer. I know the past generations would turn in their graves at the thought! But, after reading in a great GAA book 'The Throw In, And The Men That Made It', by Brendan Fullam, (these are the things that men like me can do when retired – read, write and remember!) I believe the proud tradition of the GAA will always prevail.

Incidentally, during my early football years, I had bought a new car in 1966. It was a 'Morris Minor', and it cost £490, most of which I had saved on wages of £14 per week. A full tank of petrol for it cost £1.50, and it would bring us to Dublin and back. The new car was a great asset for the matches and dances. One great year when my new car got great use was 1968 and Sligo Minor team contested the All Ireland Final. The storey was no better told than by my St. Patrick's colleague, Peadar Kearins in the GAA magazine spoken about earlier, and I relive it here for you;

The Road to Croke Park.
Peadar Kearins

Ordinary mortals will remember the summer of 1968 as one of the finest summers of modern times. Football followers of Skreen and Dromard will recall it as the most glorious summer of all times. Despite the fact that St. Pat's won their very first Senior Championship that year and that Sligo Senior footballers reached their first league semi-final, pride of place will always be to the Sligo Minor team of that year. Four St. Pat's players were members of that great Minor team who started the year as 'No hopers' and finished up losing the All-Ireland final by just one point.

Very little was expected from the Minor team that year, and with three defeats from four games in the Connaught Minor League, our confidence as we approached the championship was at an all time low. One trial game and one or two training sessions, were all the preparations we had before the first game against Mayo. The game was played on a Friday evening and the team was not picked until we arrived in the dressing room. To the surprise and delight of everyone concerned, Sligo turned in a powerful performance and emerged winners on a score of 3-5 to Mayo's

Our win over Mayo left us with just two weeks to prepare for the Connaught final against Galway. And, in that time no stone was left unturned in order to have the team in top shape. McHale Park was the venue for the final and as Sligo Minors took the field on that beautiful sunny day, they were attempting to bridge nineteen year gap.

It is history now that Sligo minors turned in another marvellous display and finished with four points to spare on a score of 1-8 to Galway's 0-7. All the St. Pat's players on the team played brilliantly and with the Connaught Crown under our belt our thoughts immediately turned to Croke Park. It was with near total disbelief that we started back training the following week, because despite the fact that we had won the Connaught Championship, the thought of playing in the All-Ireland semi-final was beyond our wildest dream. Eamon Carney was one of the five men in charge of the Minors that year and his green Morris Minor made many runs to Sligo for the next month carrying the St. Pat's players to training and home again. Our opposition in Croke Park would be provided by Armagh — amazingly enough, the same county that provided the opposition to Sligo Minors nineteen years previously. In 1949 Armagh came out the victors, but 1968 would prove to be a different story.

"Sligo Minors made Sunday August 18th a historic date for County Sligo GAA by beating Ulster Champions Armagh at Croke Park." So read the heading on the 'Sligo Champion' later that week. The score line of Sligo 1-6 to Armagh 1-3 was hardly a true picture of our superiority, because for the third time, Sligo had produced a display out of the top drawer.

Having overcome this hurdle there was just one more obstacle. The reigning champions and hot favourites for the All Ireland were Cork. On the 2nd September 1968, we left the Spa Hotel at 12 noon and travelled to Croke Park arriving at 12.45 p.m. The tension was mounting in the dressing room as we togged out and headed down the tunnel to the pitch. Our hopes for a good start to the game were shattered by two early Cork goals and by half time we were trailing by 2-5 to 0-3. Another Cork goal minutes after half time was enough to dishearten any team, but Sligo had other ideas. Suddenly things started to happen for Sligo, and cheered on by most of the 72,000 people, Sligo set about reducing Cork's lead. Point after point reduced the deficit and with four minutes remaining, we were four points behind. With Sligo pressing for the goal they needed, Richie Boland was fouled going through and we were awarded a penalty. Unfortunately, the confusion over the penalty wasted valuable minutes and *though scoring the penalty, the final whistle sounded from the kick off and our gallant effort had failed by just one point.*

For the four St. Pat's players Jimmy Kilgallon, Richie Boland, Peadar Kearins and John Kilgannon the bitter disappointment was eased somewhat one month later by winning a County Senior Championship Medal. This, combined with the All-Ireland Runners-Up Medal and the Connaught Medal, served to complete a memorable year.

During my active GAA life, Pauline and myself got married, in 1969. Naturally, it was intertwined with GAA affairs. At the time our club colleague, Brian Conlon, was just ordained a Priest in Maynooth and he was the obvious choice to marry us. His first wedding was to marry Michael and Frances Kearins in June and we were his second wedding to celebrate in August. But we forgot to seek the permission of our local Parish Priest, until the last minute. He was very irate when we told him that Father Brian was marrying us. He said to me, *"What does that 'whipper-snapper' know about it?"* and proceeded to inform us that he had to be paid also. That sounded ok, as Father Brian would not be looking for money. So, we put £10.00 in an envelope and gave it to him for the 'Letter of Freedom'. But alas, he sent it back to me and said it was *"not enough"*.

The next hitch was our wedding reception venue. We had it booked well in advance. The hotel was owned by Joe McMorrow, our GAA County Board Chairman. As one would expect, it was all football conversation with us. But the affable Joe forgot to enter the 9th of August in his booking diary. Luckily my efficient Bride to be, Pauline, made sure to double check the arrangements a few weeks prior to the wedding.

THE PROUDEST DAY OF MY LIFE - 9TH AUGUST 1969

Gerry Maye (RIP) Bestman, Myself and Pauline, Kathleen Kennedy (Pauline's sister and Bridesmaid)

Joe, being the diplomat he was, persuaded the couple whom he had double booked, to relocate their wedding to another Strandhill hotel. I also remember the cost of the reception for 110 people was £119.

I also recall all the tricks and carry-on that we received on the day. But, I will not recall them here. I also remember our honeymoon in Kerry, which we had to cut short because my mother fell ill.

Throughout my playing and management career, we won fifteen county titles with Saint Patrick's. The time had come for us to try and provide our own pitch. As for the previous hundred years, since sporting events became popular and entertaining, local, big, flat fields, where identified as the venue for them.

As Gaelic games were played in our parish, as in any other parish in the whole of rural Ireland, it was only in large towns that playing surfaces were provided. In all rural areas like Skreen and Dromard, we had to rely on the generosity of farmers with the big flat field to allow the local young people to play there. The field we had was owned by Dr O'Connor, who had played for Skreen in his younger days. But, such fields were not appreciated by the young and old, who took it all for granted.

As part of our modern progression, the field owner's insurance concerns were made known to us. The Ireland of 'take for granted' was coming to an end, and 'a wink was as good as a nod to a blind horse'. Also, at the time the GAA was pushing and encouraging every club in the country to have its own grounds – preferably, vested in the GAA - so that in future years no legal dispute could arise about its ownership.

As my club had the same vision for the future for young people, it was time to start looking for a permanent home. Some of the older members knew where there were suitable fields in the parish that games were played on in previous times. But, us *'young guns'* said it must be in a central position between the two parishes of Skreen and Dromard. We approached some farmers, but for different reasons, we were finding it impossible to hit on exactly what we needed.

I have to say that *'Lady Luck'* was on our side, as our club was on the crest of the wave, winning so many Senior Championships prior to 1982. A farm became available in the very heart of the parishes that prompted shrewdness to be able to acquire the acreage that we needed. The most important point of the matter was that the executors of the Will, namely Pat Brady and John Greer, were most accommodating to our position of acquiring the acreage and at a price that we could come up with. Naturally, in the early eighties, people's thinking was starting to move in different directions. GAA people had to be more flexible than heretofore and be more community minded than our previous generations were. The more senior members thought that the club should not join with anybody else in purchasing the ten acres, which was made available to us at a nominal price of £8,000.00. But, us *'young fellows'* knew that huge efforts had to be put into it to bring our dream to fruition.

Skreen & Dromard Community Centre in it's infancy in 1982

Our Community Council was formed at that point to help *'strengthen our hand'*, as it were and to enable each and every organization to get a share of the cake and the maximum benefit. This was a major step forward and we knew everyone must be *'singing off the same hymn sheet'* and the more senior members were overruled. One man said he *"would never stand in it"*, and another man said, *"the condition of the soil was not drainable"* and the best thing we could do was to sell it, but we knew that was not an option. From my point of view, it could not be better and modern ways would leave it perfect. This turned out to be the case I am proud to recall. Our club opened its own pitch in 1984, the Centenary of the GAA and Paddy Buggy, a Kilkenny man, who was President of the GAA at the time, opened it on the 27th May, 1984, with a senior football challenge between Sligo and Donegal. On that evening I remember saying to one of our clubmen that there was, *"something badly wrong with me, as I cannot speak properly"* and that my GAA days would have to be curtailed.

Skreen & Dromard Community Centre in 2000
I credit Eamon Burke and the Centre Committee for their progress since.

12

Humour and Wit of My Era

Like all teenagers, we grew older and one local girl who became twenty one had a party in her home. Naturally all us *good boys* were invited and her boyfriend was one of us. The fun of partying continued until five or six in the morning until it dawned on us that we had to go home and get up in time for Mass the next morning.

As I drove my Morris Minor with the 'boys' to their home areas I had the good luck to kill a fox that jumped out on the road as was usual in our area. At the time there was a bounty to be claimed if a land owner brought a fox to the barracks and the Garda certified it dead and cut the tongue out so that it could not be claimed a second time by some others of the 'boys' for more bounty which was the huge sum of 17 shillings and 6 pence. This was joy and I was not long hopping out and putting the dead fox in the boot of my car.

Next morning, Sunday, we were all at Mass as usual and the boys always stood out at the church gate after Mass. Shamie Donegan, being the top trickster among us, had a bright idea to come out from Mass early and set about dressing the fox in my football jersey and togs and propping him up with his paws on the steering wheel of my car.

So when we all came out and my good religious mother saw the new sight facing her, she went pale with shock and straight away quizzed me all about the fox. Naturally the 'boys' were all near by and she decked straight away that it was Shamie who did it. All she said was *"isn't he the rascal."* Anyway I wore the jersey and togs that day for the match. I remember the 'boys' called me the fox, but Thank God the name did not stick to me, I got my bounty money for the fox and we won the match and as we always say *"all's well that ends well"*.

I could recall lots of tricks played on people in our church by the above mentioned *good boys*. That time all men wore large overcoats with belts which were not always buttoned or belted. So when Shamie was kneeling behind one of them he would inevitably rebuckle the belt around the back of the seat and when the man then went to stand up at the appropriate part of Mass he would be restrained by the belt and totally embarrassed. Another way was to tie his two boot lacers together and he was restrained, also.

That time confession once a month was the order, always twice on a Saturday, at twelve o'clock and eight o'clock. The 'good boys' always had fun even though it was a very reverened occasion, between listening to what absolution people got and watching their red faces as they exited the confessional box, and the length of time it took a person to say their penance.

Of course when we are talking about tricksters, I would have to admit that I was up there with the best of them myself. One day while working on a house near the main road, beside the community centre, I met Sonny Brady who used always be 'jibing' us about girlfriends. He had moved from his old residence to a new one a mile down the road, but his farm was still at the old place.

Everyday he passed by where I was working and always had a dry comment. One day he left a bag inside the wall, where I was working, and went in the direction of Skreen Post Office. I guessed what he had in the bag was eggs and when he disappeared from view I took out the eggs and replaced them with stones leaving roughly the same weight in the bag. Later Sonny came back from the Post Office, picked up his bag and left to go home. Half an hour later he came rushing back, shouting at me *"where is me eggs?"* I told him that he left them behind him and not to be *"so dry"* with me the next time. This was the way at the time as the saying goes *'to get my own back'.*

Another time when one of the "good boys" and I were cycling in the dark without any light and we had the misfortune to meet the *'guards'.* The night was dark so we quickly turned and went back the other way. Naturally, the guard loved a chase and came racing after us on his bicycle of course complete with lights. He had no idea that he was trying to catch up with two very fit young men. When we got a slight distance ahead we pulled in at a gate way and it was great fun to hear him whizzing by. No summons that night!

An old lady that I knew, Mrs Conlon, told me that she used to go to dances up in a loft of a grain store. But underneath the dance floor would be packed with turf as a safety precaution as the loft floor was a bit rotten and there was a fear that it might collapse with the dancing.

Another trick was to tie a black spool of thread to the knocker of a door and stand at the turf stack, then pull the thread and someone would come to the door thinking there had been a knock at the door.

A different trick was played on a man in Dunmoran who went visiting his neighbours. The "good boys" knew his routine, so they put his donkey into the kitchen, harnessed him, took the wheels off the cart outside, took cart and wheels separately into the kitchen, reassembled the cart and attached the cart to the donkey. When the man returned he could not understand how the donkey and cart had got into the house. Just for the record - I was not involved in the last two tricks but they did happen as my father in law, Willie Kennedy, told me. There are many more tricks but we will not say any more about them.

Willie told me a story about him going to confession. Naturally, when his Protestant neighbour died he went to the funeral. The church laws at the time were that Catholics could not enter a Protestant church. If they did, it was a mortal sin and only the Bishop could give you absolution, but Willie did not know that. He told the priest in confession about entering the church, he even explained that it had started to rain and that they were getting wet. It did not work with the priest who said he would have to go to the Bishop for absolution. Willie challenged him about that point and said how would he get to Ballina to the Bishop's Palace when he *"had only a bad bicycle"*? But the priest told him that he did not care how he got to Ballina but he could not do anything for him anyway. Willie took a chance on getting into heaven without the Bishop. My experience of Willie was one of the very best and he was one of nature's gentlemen. Willie was a great storyteller and always '*told it as it was*'.

13

1974 St Patrick's GAA Tour of North America

My club St. Patrick's were invited to visit America in the 1970's. After one aborted attempt 1974 was the year that it turned out to be *'all systems go'*. Firstly, the main priority was to go as County Champions and also that our 'All Star player Micheal Kearins would be our main attraction in getting the Irish Americans to swell in numbers through the turnstiles. Prior to going we did win the Sligo Senior Championship beating Tourlestrane by one point. It was a major achievement and a very poignant one so near the trip. I was the side-line manager to Michéal Kearins when he was on the field in that County Final in Ballymote.

So on the 18th September 1974 we flew to New York for what turned out to be one of the highlights of any footballer's career. We played three games in New York, Hartford and Philadelphia and my very last occasion to play football was in Gaelic Park, New York. (My wife Pauline was one of the three ladies who made the trip also.) Incidentally, the full return fare charged by Aer Lingus was £110 per person. However, the total subsidised cost to each of the 18 players was just £30 for the three weeks, as a result of our fund-raising activity prior to the trip.

On the tour, I was able to visit my last remaining Aunt, Aunt Molly in New Jersey. All my Father's brothers and sisters (nine in total) all had emigrated and lived in the States and were deceased by 1974 apart from Molly.

We received great hospitality from my first cousins. It was a memorable three weeks and I could easily dedicate a substantial part of my memoirs to the funny happenings which occurred on that one trip alone.

I now want to add an article written by my good colleague Jimmy Kilgallon, our star club and county half-back, who was playing superbly at the time for our club, St. Patricks. I can pay him no better tribute than to quote from the prologue to his article in the 1984 souvenir booklet of the official opening of St. Patrick's GAA pitch;

> *"One of the most loyal members of Saint Patrick's club, Jimmy Kilgallon, has given sterling service to the Club and County over the last two decades. An accomplished half-back and mid-fielder, he has played in practically every position for Saint Pat's in some great matches. He has a reputation throughout the county for sportsmanship, honest and persistent endeavour and for continuous performances of remarkable consistency. An*

unfortunate series of injuries has cut short his playing career. He was one of the main organizers of the U.S. tour."

St. Pat's U.S.A. Tour – 1974
By Jimmy Kilgallon

"The old phrase, "If at first you don't succeed, try again," took on a new meaning for a small group of people, myself included on a grey October morning back in 1974. As we boarded the coach that would take us to Shannon Airport, the St. Pat's team and their loyal supporters travelling with them, were about to succeed where we failed four years previously. The St. Pat's team of 1974 were more accustomed to success than failure. In a period of eight years prior to 1974 St. Pat's contested seven county finals, six senior and one junior and failed on only one occasion to achieve victory.

Our great goal of travelling to the USA would present some major obstacles but these were overcome and our dream finally became a reality. After the bitter disappointment of having to cancel our first proposed tour of the USA in 1970, due to a dispute between the GAA Authorities in Dublin and New York, we were praying for better luck this time. Eamon Burke was the inspiration and driving force behind all our efforts to organise the tour. Having lived in the USA for ten years it remained his great desire to see a Sligo team especially St. Pat's play in 'Gaelic Park'. A small but very hard working and dedicated committee was set up to organise fundraising and finalise all travel arrangements. The generosity of the people of the parish and the many dances held in Doonflin School all helped to ease the financial burdens of the tour. While this was taking place at home another great supporter of St. Pat's resident in the USA, Tom McGuire, had thrown his weight and great influence behind the tour. As our coach pulled away from the Coragh Dtonn on that October morning, we knew only one small problem had to be solved before we stepped on the plane. As our travelling party was not large enough to charter a plane of our own, we joined with a club from Kerry called Na hAghasigh and we would all travel as one tour party. Everything went OK at Shannon as we joined with our Kerry friends, boarded the jet and headed off across the Atlantic. As we flew over the Statue of Liberty and on to John F. Kennedy Airport, the thought of St. Pat's finally playing on American soil would soon become a reality. A large crowd of people were awaiting our arrival and they gave us a tremendous welcome. Many of our touring party had relations and friends living in New York and they all turned up to greet us. Tom McGuire was there also and he had a coach waiting to take us to our hotel. The hotel was in a part of New York called Yonkers and that was our base for most of the three weeks we spent in the USA.

Our first game was on the Sunday after we arrived, Oct. 20th and our opposition was provided by the team from Kerry that we travelled out with. On Saturday we all went to Gaelic Park to take a look at the famous ground. The weather was very cold that evening and the football pitch was showing the signs of wear due to the heavy summer programme but we all had a few kicks just to get the feel of things.

When we arrived at Gaelic Park on Sunday, it seemed like every Sligo person in New York had come along to see us. People whom we had never met and some we never heard of came up to us to say how proud they were to be able to cheer for a Sligo team. St. Pat's took the field at approx. 3 p.m. on that Sunday. It hardly crossed our minds that we were creating our own bit of history. We were the first Sligo team in the history of GAA to cross the Atlantic to play in Gaelic Park. Our game turned out to be a tough Baptism for us, but despite the fact that we were behind at half time we got into our stride in the second half and recorded a great victory. After the game our captain M. Kearins was presented with a lovely trophy, so our tour had got off to the perfect start and hopefully we could keep it up.

Our first full week was left mainly free of football or social functions so that anyone in our party who had relations or friends in New York whom we wanted to visit could do so. For those who did not go visiting, sightseeing was the order of the day. A twenty seat bus was hired for the duration of our tour and with Eamon Burke at the wheel and Tom McGuire giving details of where we were and where we were going, we did not have many dull moments. While on the subject of visiting people in New York I could not let this opportunity pass without paying tribute to all the people, many of them total strangers to us, who called to our hotel and invited us back to their homes for beautiful meals. Of all the people that extended invitations and generosity to us, and there were many, two names stand out in my memory, one is Tommy Kilgallon and the other is Denis Reynolds. Denis is a brother-in-law of Pat and Sally Brady and Tommie is a brother of Peter and Frank Kilgallon and it is not the fact that both men were strangers to us but that they each took no less than six of our party back home with them in Tommie's case for nearly two days.

The second game of our tour would take us to Hartford. By Friday night all our party had returned to our base and early on Saturday morning we set off by coach for Connecticut. On our arrival we were met by many of the Hartford GAA club and made most welcome and once again our accommodation and entertainment was excellent. On Sunday the weather was scorching hot as we lined up against the local Hartford team and again a large crowd of people turned up to see us. On a lush green pitch St. Pat's turned in one of their finest performances and won by nine or ten points. The Hartford team included three Foley brothers who had represented New York in many league finals against the top county teams in Ireland and also Mick Wright who had won All-Ireland medals with Offaly a few years previously. After the match we were taken to a reception in our honour, many glowing tributes were paid to our teams performances and our captain Micheal Kearins again received the winner's trophy.

We returned to Yonkers in the early hours of Monday morning and fell into bed very tired, but happy with the way our team was living up to the reputation we brought with us. Most nights during our tour when we were not at receptions or visiting friends nearly all our party would go along to an Irish Club in the Bronx called 'Good Time Charley's'. The resident guests every night during our stay there were Anna McGoldrick and also Two's Company. For many Irish people visiting New York this club is the place to meet all your friends who treat Charley's as a home from home. The St. Pat's team found that to be the case so when about twenty of our group joined up with Aiden and Michael McDermott from Aughris, Joe Forde and Brendan Flynn from Enniscrone and many more and threw in a few Irish songs from Anna McGoldrick, you could be forgiven for thinking we were in the Coragh Dtonn. A special thanks to the McDermott brothers for leaving their transport at our disposal day and night and during our tour and to Joe Forde also for the same.

Our third game was played in mid week against a Sligo selection in New York and again it was third time lucky for us. As Sligo had been champions of New York the previous year they provided us with stiff opposition and their team included former Sligo, Kildare, Derry players and even a former St. Pat's player.

The biggest social event of our tour was held on Friday, November 1st. The event was a marvellous Dinner Dance, held in the 'Tower View Ballroom', New York at which all our party were guests. The dance was organised by the New York committee headed by Tom McGuire, who had worked so hard to make our tour enjoyable. The ballroom was decorated in the St. Pat's colours red and green and a few hundred people mostly Sligo people but many from Leitrim, Mayo and other counties attended and all combined to give us a night we will never forget.

On Saturday morning the festivities of the previous night were put behind us as we hit the road once again for our final game. Our last game was arranged for Philadelphia and the opposition was provided by the Tyrone team in Philadelphia. A few days earlier St. Pat's received a request from John Kerry O'Donnell to try to fit in another game in Gaelic Park if at all possible.

John Kerry was head of the GAA in New York and St. Pat's agreed to allow five of their players to remain in New York and join up with the Sligo team there. Having arranged who was to travel and who was to remain, we set off on our final journey and arrived in Philadelphia by late Saturday evening.

We stayed two nights in Philadelphia and the generosity of the people there was evident from the moment we arrived. On our first night there two brothers from Leitrim called Travers, gave us the use of their premises, 'The Shamrock Club' to run a dance and all the profit went to offset our expenses. The following day, Sunday, November 3rd, we lined out against the local team and despite being under strength and playing in intense heat, we kept our 100% record and eventually won by two points. Later that evening, our touring party were guests at a steak dinner and cocktails hosted by the local GAA team. At a very enjoyable social function, following the meal I had the pleasure of receiving the winner's trophy on behalf of the St. Pat's team. Next morning we were on the road again, this time Washington D.C. was our destination.

Despite the fact that we had only one day in that great city we did manage to see many of its famous landmarks. Our first stop had to be the 'White House' and we were lucky enough to catch a glimpse of the then President, Gerald Forde. Our tour around the city took us to many famous monuments, erected in memory of former U.S. Presidents and mention of the late President John F. Kennedy always reminds us of our visit to 'Arlington Cemetery'. Everyone that goes to see Arlington cemetery likes to have their photo taken standing beside the eternal flame that burns over the late President's grave, and all our party did likewise. The grave of the late Bobby Kennedy and 'Tomb of the Unknown Soldier' were some of the memories we took with us as we left that historic place of rest.

Arriving back at Yonkers late Monday night we knew our tour had only a few days left to run and even the three ladies, Frances Kearins, Carmel Clarke and my sister, Maureen who travelled to every game we played in *the USA, were starting to feel slightly jaded. To cap a great weekend, the players that stayed in New York won their game also, so having arrived out as champions we would be returning home with a proud record. Our last days were spent shopping and saying farewell to our relations and many friends we had met.*

By lunch time on Wednesday our cases were packed, then loaded on the coach and we checked out of the Yonkers Hotel. Our flight home went according to plan as did our coach trip from Shannon. A cavalcade of cars and flags met us at Ballisadare and escorted our coach to the Coragh Dtonn and all our families and friends had turned up to give us a rousing reception. In concluding, I would like to thank everybody who helped to make our tour possible and to the people at home and in the USA whose names I should have mentioned and didn't, please accept my apology. To Tom McGuire for his arrangement of the accommodation, the games we played in various cities in the USA and the many functions laid on for us and to Eamon Burke for all his hard work we will be always indebted."

County Sligo Person of the Year 1991
Standing at Back from left: Ted Nealon (T.D.), John McGettrick, P J Murphy (Chairman of the National Mental Health Association), Mattie Brennan (T.D.), Rita Flannery, Sean McManus (Mayor of Sligo), Brian Devaney, Donal O'Shea (CEO N.W.H.B.), Paddy Conway (Chairman Sligo County Council), Seamus Finn (Editor, Sligo Champion), Paul Byrne (Manage, Sligo County Council)
Seated from left: Marie Claude Ward, Ina Monaghan, Vera Taheny, Joe Crotty, Bridie Rodgers, Tom Roddy (County Sligo Person of the Year 1991), Mary Weir, Eamon Carney, Jim Lawlor

ST. PATRICK'S TEAM PHOTOGRAPH IN YONKERS, NEW YORK 1974

Seated left to right; Michael Farrell, Michael Boland, James Kearins, Micheal Kearins (Captain), Declan Foley, John Tempany, Peadar Kearins, Jimmy Kilgallon.
Standing; Tom McGuire (New York Tour Director), Thomas Mahon, Edward Rush, James Kilcullen, Stanley Clarke, Noel Kearins, Josie Boland, Eamon Carney, Leo Boland and Eamon Burke (Irish Tour Director).
The ladies who travelled with us at the time were; Frances Kearins, Pauline Carney, Kathleen Donegan, Maureen Kilgallon and Carmel Clarke (then Cahill)

My father in law Willie Kennedy playing his fiddle on his last night in his own house and three weeks before he died on 16th July 1996

14

All My Illnesses and Finally Multiple Sclerosis (M. S.) in 1988

I was twenty-six in 1966, and my girlfriend, Pauline, who was nursing in Jervis Street Hospital, was shocked when I told her that I had a bad pain in my head. Naturally, Saint Patrick's Team was playing in a tournament on the Sunday before and I got a severe knock. There was no 'free' awarded, as that was not in the rulebook at that time. An opposing player could illegally hit his opponent in possession of the ball.

This is what happened to me. As I kicked the ball towards goal, I was put spinning, and my head hit the ground. No doubt, I felt pulling in my neck and I saw stars. Still I recovered because no one faked injury at the time or Joe Cuffè, our big mid-fielder would call you *"Mr. Softy"*, the name of a famous racehorse at the time. I remember a fellow wearing a support bandage. I recall Padraic McMunn having a piece of cloth round his knee, and Cuffe mocked him. The 'hamstring' was unheard of at the time. The only ham we knew about was the ham that was the shoulder meat of the pig.

Anyway, we won that tournament, beating Dromahair in the final in Mullaney's field in Sooey. Incidentally, there was a carnival in Boyle and it seemed the right place to go that night to celebrate. Micheal Kearins had his father's car, so we had a great night. But when I tried to get out of the car in the early hours of Monday morning, I had to get pulled out of it. Still, it was work as usual in the morning, in my Morris Minor, to Collooney, where Scanlons were building a girls National School.

I had the pain in my head all that morning, and I used to put my head against the wall for relief. I remember saying to the funniest man on the job, Tommy Conway of Kilmacowen, that if the pain was as bad tomorrow I would not be able to come to work. That is what happened. It was the worst headache that anyone could imagine. I could not recall the football knock at the time. Anyway, it would not sound right to say, *"I got hurt playing football"*. The next day the pain was still bad and I had to stay at home. My mother sent for the Doctor and he came and looked at me and said I had 'Sinusitis', and to get up and go for a spin on the bicycle. I could not see where I was going, but still, I got up when he said it.

As it turned out I had a school colleague, Michael Coleman, who was home on holidays from England and staying in Enniscrone and I had planned to go and see him. As my driving was not so good, with the pain, I brought along my good friend, Padraic Kilcullen. We met Michael Coleman, but I could not talk to him for many minutes, only reaching across the wall vomiting. We drove home, and I let Padraic out at his turn-off on the main road and came home. I left my car halfway on the road outside my house, ran in and lay on the sofa in agony. The next morning my mother got the doctor again and he recommended that I go to hospital. My mother went to our good neighbour, Maureen Kearins, who got her car to bring me to hospital. This was the worst journey of my life, as I had to get out of the car a few times to vomit.

At the hospital, they put dark glasses on me and they bandaged around my head. My mother was distracted, but I did not know how bad I was. Then, Pauline who was a student Nurse came from Dublin to see me – imagine, she was only nineteen and I was twenty two. Then two good Nurses called Maeve Gorman and Celia Coleman, whom Pauline and I knew, both said that I was very bad and unconscious at times. It must have been decision time then, because I recall seeing a Priest at my side, and a candle lit beside my bed and my mother crying for me, her only son. I saw a lovely white corridor, but I did not know where it was going.

Then, I remember the ambulance journey. It was very uncomfortable and very bumpy. The nurse told me, afterwards that she stopped the ambulance driver at her house on Pearse Road in Sligo to get Holy Water, as she thought I would not survive the journey. I remember a nurse getting me to make it an 'X' on a form and I was told I was in theatre. That was all I remembered for days. I remember looking at an unfamiliar ceiling and I discovered I had no hair and my head was in a bandage and that I was in the Richmond Hospital in Dublin.

One of my first memories, as I came to, in a few days, was of seeing Micheal Kearins and Donal O'Connor (another team-mate of mine at the time). They were at my bedside. I said to them, *"Tell my mother I'll be ok"*. Apparently, I had a brain haemorrhage, had four 'burr holes' in my head, the clot drained and I was on the road to recovery. It was great to see Pauline every day little did I know why. She told me, afterwards, why she was able to be at my bedside. She was on night duty, got up to see me, and unwittingly broke hospital rules and then told the Matron about it, only to be told she was suspended and had to leave. Even though she was not on duty, she stayed in the nurses' home, but, after four weeks she told her cousin, Micheal Kearins, about her plight. As he was a quick, smart Dubliner who incidentally, played in a band, he arranged a meeting with the Matron, and reminded her of her responsibilities to a young girl. Pauline was back on duty the next day.

Even though everybody prayed and was very good to my mother, they never let her see me in hospital. Pauline kept her informed about me. The first glimpse she got of me was when I came home on the train to Collooney, after seven weeks in the hospital. Herself and Maureen Kearins were there to meet me and took me home.

Then it was 'get on with it time' again. I started to drive again, but I was told not to play football again. I was anxious and tempted to get playing again and played junior. I was told, lately that the lads on the Ballisadare team were told to *"Keep away from Carney, as he has a bad head"*. As it turned out it was a clash with a Ballisadare player in a junior match, in 1973, on our home pitch called 'Dan's Field' that finished football for me. As I caught the ball and turned to kick it, I got an elbow in the nose. It was sore and bled a bit, but it was only when I looked in the car mirror on togging in, that I knew it was broken – it was at a slight angle to my face. So when I came home and had my supper, I told Pauline, *"I must go to hospital and get this nose straightened"*. That was the last match for me as the she *'tore strips off me'*. We had four small children at the time and it was only when I was kept four days in the hospital that I realized she was right. One of my good team-mates used to say, *"It's not when the fans start asking when? But why?"* – Shamie Donegan, the wittiest man on the team.

My second health problem happened at the age of 28. I was working like a 'Trojan', I was only nine and a half stone, but with a pain around my heart area. I doubted that there must be something wrong with me. I decided to go to the Mobile Chest Unit that was at Sligo Town Hall. I brought two young workers, who worked for me at the time, namely Thomas Mahon and Michael Gallagher, with me (*possibly to make myself not look too bad*). With the x-ray over it was back to work as quickly as possible.

The next day went well as all working days did. When I came home at seven o'clock, I knew there was something badly wrong. Pauline and my mother were very distressed and told me straight away that I have to go to hospital the next day. And they told me the choice was Peamount in Dublin or Merlin Park in Galway. *"What?"* I said, *"Sure! I can't go that soon.*

What about the work?" They replied, *"It's not your say is on it"*. The Infectious Disease Doctor had come to our house that day, told them it was very serious and the family would have to be investigated also. As Pauline did not drive at the time and we had two young children, she got a pal of mine Frank Leonard, to drive me and herself to Merlin Park.

I'll never forget that experience, leaving on a brilliant sunny day and being put into bed in a T.B. Ward with about ten men. In fact the man in the bed next to me, got out of bed, misbehaved on the floor beside me, got back into bed and died. All I could do was pull the sheets over my head and sleep. I also wondered as the ceiling seemed to be covered in cobwebs, all hanging like icicles and very thick. This must have been something to do with a T.B. cure.

Anyway I got the same drugs as the rest of the patients. As Dr Keyes, the TB Specialist, was on her rounds in a few days, she paid special notice to me and said, *"I don't think you have T.B. We will have to do further tests"*, and ordered that I be moved to a Side Ward. At this time, I was petrified, and thought I had Cancer on my lungs instead. A test involved taking a piece of gland from between my neck and shoulder to be analyzed. Little did I know that the test would have to be carried out in England. I kept asking the nurses, each day, if the results were back. I can honestly say it was like a death sentence waiting for the results and the worst feeling of the 'unknown', I suppose. The other thing I remember was that a clerical student was in the bed next to me. Francis Judge was his name, and he was reading his Missal, most of the time – now Father Francis Judge a native of Castleconnor.

Finally to conclude about my Diagnosis, the results came back to say I had not T.B., but 'Sarcoidosis', that I had to be put on steroids and have chest x-rays every month. I was warned not to go near dust or I would be dead within twelve months. Thank God, it worked out well since. It was the result of me inhaling fiberglass in the course of my work, with no safety precautions such as masks being used in 1975, which was recommended, straightaway by Dr Keyes. She also said to me to wear a mask at hay foddering, which I did, but with great inconvenience.

As per usual, that illness cleared itself through the next few years, and my weight went from nine and a half stone to my normal thirteen stone, until I found myself clumsy and unsteady in 1984. This remained the situation for the next four years, through the most horrific period of my lifetime. Even though my good wife, Pauline, had me investigated through a specialist in 1987, he did not think there was something wrong with me, so I persisted with my construction activities and what I thought could be a normal life. Alas, people who knew me, made various comments to me over those horrible years.

Some of the comments made to me when I was going downhill in those years were; once a fellow, using a urinal beside me in a hotel, looked at me and said, *"Be God! You're holding your own"*. The only answer I could make was, *"and so are you, too!"* Another fellow, that I met at a funeral, said, *"Be God! You're not so bad. You were dying ten years ago."* Another time, when I went to a clinic with Pauline – the Nurse said to her, *"Do you want to go inside with your father?"*

Another time when I was building a brick fireplace in a pub, two fellows came in for a 'hailer' in the morning, after the night before. When they saw me going behind the polythene hoarding that I had erected to keep the dust away from the customers, one of the fellows said to the other, *"Poor old Carney is f**ked"* and continued to discuss me. They did not realize that this polythene was not soundproof, and that I could hear it all – two men who are dead now, God rest them!

Yet another time, when I was working on scaffolding at the front of a house, a slightly intoxicated man came in to talk to us. He asked where I was from and I said, *"Sure! You should know me. I'm from Dromard."* So, then he proceeded to talk about the great football team we had, talked about Micheal Kearins, Padraic McMunn, Joe Cuffe and Shamie Donegan. And, I said, *"Do you not know me?"* He looked a bit closer, and shook his head. Then, I took off my cap, and his comment was: *"Oh! Carney, you f**ker you! I thought you were dying a few years ago"*. All we had after that was a good laugh.

The next time I felt embarrassed was when I was in a corpse house or at a funeral and a few old ladies were talking together I would hear them as I passed them. And, the comment would be, *"Look at poor old Eamon Carney! God help him!"* It was nice, if I was out of earshot, those times. Other embarrassing moments where when I was asked to speak at a dinner dance. My voice was slurred and the words would not come out as I expected they should. Sometimes I would hear people snigger and make uncomfortable moves in their seat.

Other frustrating moments were when I was stopped by Gardaí on a few occasions. Once, a Garda saw me getting into my car at the 'Park Hotel' in Sligo, thought I was drunk and, naturally, stopped me as I approached the road-side, only to be told by my colleague, Jimmy Kilcullen, in no uncertain terms, that I never drank alcohol. Another time, when I was driving a bit slow, in a replacement car, with my daughter, Sinead, a Garda stopped me to check for alcohol. Naturally Sinead was irate with him, and told him so. Those are some of the pitfalls to hit me in my undiagnosed years, plus losing a lot of money from my negligence, due to stress through those stressful years.

A 'Cat-Scan' was the only means of diagnosis, even though Pauline knew that it was probably MS that I had. At one stage, a Specialist told us about an MRI Scanner that was capable of diagnosing but the nearest one of its kind was in Hamburg, in Germany. We were told there might be a unit introduced to Ireland in the late eighties. Eventually, the first one appeared in Ireland, in the Mater Hospital. We were told the massive cost of it and that it was only in the private hospital. But I could be wheeled across to it.

So, on the 18th March, 1989, after the Specialist Dr Staunton, read the x-ray, he announced to me that I had MS. I simply asked him would I be able to work again. *"Ah! You might!"* he said and kept going. I cried for two hours. But when I reflected on the relief of actually knowing what the name of my illness was, I came to terms with the fact that I would keep going until the bitter end.

Coming to terms with Multiple Sclerosis is difficult to describe – no backup service as I will describe later. A 'Rehab' man called one day, and told me about their services. But I could not see much logic in his talk. Anyway he smoked cigarettes non-stop and he just seemed to be bored with his job. Then a nurse friend of Pauline called Fidelma Hanley, told her what she heard was available by way of support.

Then she heard from somebody else about a 'disabled grant' to suit my forthcoming requirements. It was post-haste to get on with that side of it. I set about building my disabled room and got door frames widened to suit a wheelchair. I did not feel too bad about it. I had made up my mind that I would beat my problem.

What happens when a 'tea totaler' falls asleep and family plays tricks

15

My Change of Lifestyle to Stonemasonry

For the next few months after coming home from the Mater, I reflected on what I might be able to do with my life. I did a restoration job on a horse-tub trap, which I had stored in my workshop. I also thought craftwork might suit. Making spinning wheels was one of my thoughts. But, my dexterity wasn't great and anyway, workshop life would not be suitable for my mentality, which was as an outdoor worker all my life.

While sitting at my kitchen table pondering one day, I looked at the beautiful vista of the Ox Mountains and Carna Gloc (Carrownaglogh, the large farm in front of my window), God inspired me to re-build the unsightly stone wall that hindered my view. I took the spade, shovel, briar hook and set about clearing the briars and re-building it. As I worked at that wall in 1989, a good agricultural reclamation contractor called, John McDaniel, of Ballisadare stopped to talk to me. He admired the job I was doing on the wall and said to me that he knew of a man in Ballisadare who wanted to get a new stone wall built, but did not know anyone capable of doing it.

My first stone wall in 1989

So without realising the emphasis that would be put on stonework in the coming years, I built Gerry Tague's entrance. For the next fourteen years I enjoyed working for people who knew me and who realised I had a problem, but were fully aware they would have a good job done for them.

One of the first builders to place his faith me was Paddy Egan of Ballymote. He was restoring Maugherow Church in North Sligo, which had been struck by lightening for a second time, exactly one hundred years to the day after the first strike. At first I was a bit reluctant to tackle such a major (rock-face) cut stone job. Still Paddy had confidence in me and guaranteed me that he would "keep me right."

Sure enough I had a slight difficulty at the start of the job, but I overcame that the second day. As Paddy was a great tradesman himself I got great experience of top quality work. One of Paddy's stories was about a competition he had in his younger years between himself and another block layer as to which of them would build the most blocks in a day. The other fellow worked far harder than Paddy and had finished way ahead of him.

He was bragging and teasing Paddy about not being as good a man as him. Paddy who remained *'cool calm and collected'*, smoked his pipe, replied and remarked to him,

"When you would have your block work all taken down, and the damp course put in as you should have under the first course of blocks and then re-built, I will be at home and have my dinner eaten, my paper read and be gone to bed."

That was his teaching lesson never to be forgotton by that fellow! There is an old saying *'The more hurry the less speed'*. Or, as I would often say myself to young apprentices: *"There is no substitute for thinking".* (Thank you Paddy for good memories)

I'm proud to say that in that time I also trained a lot of young men who have gone on to successful careers in stonemasonry. I'm proud to name them here - Tommy Gordon, Martin Kilcullen, Noel Burns, Aiden Hegarty, Francis Costelloe, Pat Kilgallen and Anthony Cawley as well as some Latvian boys, Pasia and Sashia, Evard and Euris *(I hope they will forgive me if I have not spelled their names entirely correctly).*

I'd like to take this opportunity to pay tribute to all those people who put their faith in me at that difficult time of my career.

Unfortunately, my happy time as a Stonemason was cut short on the 15th February 2004, when I fell at our MS Therapy Centre. On the day, I had attended a presentation at the Centre and was leaving to return to my work when I fell straightforward in huge pain. Up to that point I enjoyed fourteen great years building stone. But from that day forward my life's journey changed. The x-ray that evening showed that there was nothing broken. If nothing was broken I thought it was not too bad, as the doctor did not indicate that there was any serious problem. But, still, no driving, no sleeping at night and 'Sore! Sore! Sore!' was the entry in my Diary for two years after that and no work, ever again!

After months of enduring this agony, my first visit was for an assessment and then I had to wait for an MRI, three weeks later, to see the Shoulder Specialist in the Blackrock Clinic, to be told that I had ruptured tendons in my shoulder and that I was too old to have them repaired. Apparently over fifty is too old for tendons to adhere to the bone. Bad news again! No work ever again at my beloved stonework and I had to sit at home moaning and groaning - a bit. That Specialist referred me to the Pain Control Doctor in Sligo General Hospital, a Dr. Fitzgerald. My meeting and consultation with him improved my chances, as he referred me to Dr. Macey, the Orthopaedic Surgeon who worked in Sligo General Hospital, for a second opinion. When he saw my x-rays he straightaway said that he would repair my ruptured tendons which he duly did, with considerable success.

From Sligo General Hospital to an enjoyable recovery in Our Lady's Hospital in Manorhamilton - (where I enjoyed the hospitality of so many Leitrim people) - that was another painful period of my life endured. Incidentally, while in hospital I missed the death of Pope John Paul II and the election of Pope Benedict XVI. Prince Rainer of Monaco died and Prince Charles got married. All the time my shoulder was getting better and the pain became more bearable, for which I am grateful. I thank God for the skill of the Surgeon, Dr Macey.

So, between physiotherapy and tablets, forgetting to take them, the journeys to the Chiropractor and to the Shoulder Specialist, in the Blackrock Clinic, that was the end of my stoneworking life. That is how my memoir writing started as part of my Occupational Therapy.

The first all-stone house I built
Photograph shows Patrick Carter, owner and Tom Currid, Contractor

The last stone house I built for Daragh & Collette Mulvey,
proudly assisted by my grandson Darragh Williams.

One of the stone jobs I did for Felix McHugh (Contractor)

Felix McHugh (Builder) and Myself nearing
the end of his Castle Dargan Complex. The entrance to which I was proud to restore at
the start of the project in '04

Stonework for Tom McGuinn in Drumcliffe 1990

Left to Right; Eamon Carney, Tom McGuinn, Damien Feeney, Tommie Gordon and Cyril Feeney at work

Cladding our M S Therapy Centre in 1990

Left to Right; Eamon Carney, Tommy Gordon and Martin Kilcullen

A sick father and his innocent child, Paul

My trap, restored by me in 1989

16

My Involvement in M. S. Therapy Centre at Start-Up

Our Multiple Sclerosis Therapy Centre, in Sligo is my pride and joy, as I am a founder member with my MS colleague and friend, the late, Padraic Kilcullen. I must recall my earliest involvement. Soon after I got MS in 1989, I went to seek the help of a Faith Healer which was the only option for anybody with a terminal illness. So, 'low and behold', where should Padraic and myself meet, only, in the 'Old Sheeling Hotel' in Raheny, Dublin, on St. Patrick's Day 1989. Our good wives, Pauline and Breege, had accompanied us, but neither of us knew the other had MS.

We were seeking the help of Finbar Nolan, the Faith Healer. Soon after that, Padraic and Breege heard about an MS Therapy Centre in Trim, Co. Meath. It had a Hyperbaric Oxygen Chamber and a Physiotherapy Department. Having paid a few visits to it, the Directors of the Centre, advised Padraic that travelling such long journeys, to avail of the facility, was not really that beneficial to him and would he not think to explore the possibility of getting one in his area, in Sligo. Sure enough, I was the man that Padraic first, talked to.

We called an open meeting in the 'Embassy Bar' in Sligo, to discuss the issue. We invited Mary Murray and her nurse helper, Angela, from the MS Centre in Trim. We were a bit apprehensive as to the outcome. To our surprise, a crowd of about forty people turned up and we elected a Committee on the night. Our brief from that night forward, was to explore a correct site or an existing building and to have it located in the best possible place. The location was to be the vital key to our project. We explored a lot of existing buildings and green-field sites. I spotted a building that proved to be the best available.

When I told Pauline she was a little dubious, as she said she thought it was earmarked for another project, as it was a vacant old 'cut-stone' former gardener's residence in the grounds of Saint John's Hospital. Initially we wrote to the North Western Health Board to seek and develop it. The reply we received was positive. The terms were that it would be on a ninety-nine-year lease. But if there was a cure got for MS, in the meantime, that it would revert back to the Health Board.

Fundraising would have to commence immediately. All the eight members and the Committee had a big role to play in this. Our first venture was to raffle a Volkswagen Polo car, which we got at cost price from Tommy

Parkes, the Volkswagen Dealer in Ballisodare. Tommy was very generous, as we all had played football together in our early days. Our Committee set the price at £1.00 per ticket and a big effort was put into selling them by all concerned. Through our efforts that first draw was a massive success, and gave us a great start.

Then some of the members came up with the idea of making representation to the Fianna Fàil Government of the time. We wrote to our local TD, Matt Brennan to ask him how to go about it. Matt duly made an appointment with the Minister for Health, Dr. John O'Connell. This appointment was for three weeks later. We got our portfolio together with our aims and objectives and sent a copy to him. I was the obvious Fianna Fàil man to make the journey, accompanied by Carmel McCarney, a 'Trojan' worker on our committee.

We travelled by train and walked to Hume House, the Department of Health Headquarters, to meet the Minister. That proved to be another successful visit, as the good Minister, whose Government was about to go out of Office, looked up whatever surplus funds were left in his Department. He told us that he had £10,000.00, and that he would give it to our worthy venture. This was a considerable amount of money at the time in 1989. We thanked him sincerely and wished him well in the forthcoming elections.

I produced a book of tickets for my inside pocket and explained that this was one of our fundraisers that we had started to let him know that we were serious about our project. Then he said, "Sure! I'll buy two books" and he gave us a £20.00 note. I said to him, "We're in a bit of a hurry" as we had to get the train back to Sligo, and we were on our 'last legs' to catch it. He then offered that his driver would take us to Westland Row Station, now Pearse Station. So, Carmel and myself travelled in a State Car to our destination. Dr. John O'Connell was the nicest man and I hope he read our well put together portfolio. The last thing he said to us was that he wished "more volunteers would set the same headlines" as we were setting and "get on with it, without too much form filling".

The next big fundraiser on our behalf was in conjunction with North West Radio Station. It was called, "Beat On The Street". People were asked to pledge a certain amount of money on a nominated weekend. This turned out to be a major winner for us, as the people of the entire northwest opened their hearts to us and pledged and gave us another great boost to our fundraising efforts.

Another fundraiser, which the people of the Tireragh Gun Club carried out was a sponsored bareback pony ride, with Gerry Kilgallon as 'jockey' and volunteers collecting cash in buckets. That night they held a 'big auction' in the Beach Bar, with numerous items auctioned by Brendan Howley with numerous volunteers giving of their time. I will never forget those generous people.

Our first addition and renovation job on our newly acquired building was done in record time by our builder, Tommy Horan. It was officially opened by the President of Ireland, Mary Robinson 30th July 1993. We also acquired a great, efficient Manager, Sr. Mary Henry, from North Western Health Board, who developed our facilities to a state of perfection over the next few years. As our Therapy Centre became more used, our committee felt it required another extension, but Padraic and myself were apprehensive as to whether it would be well frequented or not.

The second extension was finished by Ivan Hamilton a few years later. Still, like a lot more projects in Ireland, our Centre had to be altered and extended once more to cope with the growing numbers. This was a major job, which was totally funded by the Northwest Branch of the Construction Industry Federation, a massive gesture, never to be forgotten and was completed on time by, Felix McHugh, Building Contractor. The Opening Ceremony was performed by, yours truly, Eamon Carney, in June 2000. I still go there for therapy and Hyperbaric Oxygen once a week.

Breege and Padraic Kilcullen and myself at a fundraising function
in the Sancta Maria Hotel, Strandhill

My Involvement in M.S. Therapy Centre at Start-Up

Left to Right; Liam Hunt (MS Therapy Committee), Eamon Carney (Chairman Fundraising Committee), Tommy Horan (Chairman North West CIF), Sr. Mary Henry (Manager, North West Therapy Centre), Ray Gilboy (Director CIF) taken during the Official Opening Ceremony of our extension on 16th June 2000

Members of the Construction Industry Federation visit the complete extension of the North West MS Therapy, Ballytivnan, Sligo.
Left to Right; Micheal Keenan, Oliver Haslett, Tommy McGuire, Eamon Carney (Chairman Fundraising Committee), Pat Reynolds, Tommy Horan (Chairman North West Branch CIF), Tom Currid, Ray Gilboy (Director CIF), Seamus Cummins, Felix McHugh, Liam Kelleher (Director General CIF)

North West Therapy Centre 2000 - The finished project on which I was proud to work

17

My Travels to Lourdes, Rome, Medugorje and South Africa

As a pilgrim, I visited Lourdes on three occasions with vivid memories of the faith, devotion and peacefulness of that lovely Shrine. On one occasion, Pauline and myself flew on to Rome, (I wrote a journal about it at the time, 1981). This was the very time when Pope John Paul II had been shot and badly injured in Saint Peter's Square. The summary of the trip I made is as follows;

In remembrance of my trip to the City of Rome and the Vatican, the loveliest city in the world and surely, the most exciting, with its unique and famous architecture and art. The native people here are not very communicative or responsive, but surely are a very excitable and impatient race.

The Coliseum I found very awesome and eerie. I shall never forget my day at the Vatican and the Sistine Chapel. It is all too much to describe. The beauty of the place, especially the Sistine Chapel, with its famous Michelangelo paintings on its dome ceiling and behind the main altar. Rome, by night is beautiful, especially the Trevi Fountain and the square around it. All night dancing and eating. Our tour to Assisi, 258 miles from Rome, to see the home of Saint Francis and Saint Claire. All the beauty of the place and the hillsides of vines I will never forget. Also, the Catacombs - a must when in Rome. This is the Roman underground maze of burial chambers, which were used in the earlier centuries. The remaining, true artefacts of the crucifixion of Our Lord, and the massive stairs from Pontius Pilate's mansion, which led Our Lord on his way to his crucifixion. People have climbed this massive stairs on their knees all through the centuries. For people to get a genuine knowledge of Christianity, as opposed to learning Bible history – this is the only way to see and be part of it firsthand. I was lucky enough to have the experience of serenity on this awesome occasion.

More recently we were in Medugorje, a heavenly place, also. While there, I saw what I think is a phenomenal occurrence and also the development of the 'Peace Garden', with a huge bronze figure of the Risen Christ. It had a trickle of water coming from an area beside one of its knees. As I sat watching people holding little bottles and tissues to gather drops of the mysterious water, I at first, dismissed the fact and talked of my theory of it. I said it was condensation on the inside of the 12ft. high bronze statue, which was filling up the hollow leg and weeping out at the knee joint area. Another fellow, beside me, thought there was a hole in the head area and that rain seeped down. Then I investigated further and tested the side of the statue of the Risen Christ, to discover that it has a totally solid core – so, there goes my hypothesis. The mystery is still happening to this day.

As I wrote this Medugorje story, today, my phone rang and who should it be, but an acquaintance of mine from County Kilkenny, Michael Grogan. He and his wife, May, are avid Medugorje pilgrims, whom I got to know, as they are friends of my next door neighbours, Catherine and Dermot Finneran. They go to Megjegorie each year. May talked first, inquiring how I was and I said to her, *"You won't die this year"* (*a saying used to acknowledge the coincidence of her ringing whilst I was writing about our mutual interest in Medugorje)* and I continued, *"I am writing a story about Medugorje"*. She simply said, *"Michael is suffering badly at the moment and I will put you on to him"*. Then I told Michael what I was writing about and he said, *"That's not it all!"* He went on to tell me that he and May, along with more pilgrims, witnessed the "Sacred Heart and a Cross," in the sky over the statue of the Risen Christ. He said that they never saw anything so beautiful in their lives. I simply said, *"Can I put that in my book, Michael?"*, he replied and said, *"Why not?"* so, please God, what I have written will not fall on deaf ears. Michael is in a wheelchair and suffering, even though he was a mechanic up to a few years ago. And, all I will say is that, *"God's ways are strange ways"*.

Trips abroad are not a big deal to people anymore. But, I suppose, when I was a bit disabled, it was an extra challenge for me. My trip to Durban, South Africa, from Sligo railway station started on the 4th December 1996. It all happened due to the fact that my good friends, Colin Murphy and his wife, Maureen, had come back to live in Dromard, a few years previously, with my cousin, Tommy. (Incidentally, Colin was one of the best men ever to 'pitch-up' in Dromard – to use his own witty saying! To me and my family he could not have been a better friend. May he rest in peace.) They were going back to Durban, for (their daughter) Jill's wedding and courteously asked me would I like to go also. Sure, that offer of three weeks in the sun and a wedding, I could not afford to miss.

From Dublin, it was an early morning flight to Heathrow, with a stopover of a few hours and more importantly, all the airlines gave a great service for wheelchair bound passengers. The international air company all employ over sixty five year old gentleman to wheel and accompany awaiting disabled passengers to and from aircraft and the terminal buildings. The next stop-over was in Brussels thirty five minutes later. An hour later we took off with Sibena Airlines – *"A monster aircraft"* is how I described it and *"as big as 'Seafield ballroom' in Easkey".*

Bernard & Jill Beukes with myself on the day of their wedding in Durban

As we flew at high altitudes, with 570 passengers and approximately 500mph, I heard on the radio that Michael Lowry resigned from the Coalition Government and I read Cari Lauder's book, which she called 'Standing in the Sunshine, A Cure for MS'. I pondered to myself and said, *"Maybe, sometime I will write a book and call it 'Sitting in the Sunshine'".* We landed in Johannesburg Airport after approximately fourteen hours in the air, all of which I enjoyed - between eating, sleeping, reading and looking in amazement at the flight screen as we flew over the Sahara and the Kalahari Desserts, Kitwe and Zambia, the mountain ranges, cities and all this seen from the air. Imagine forty eight wheelchair-bound people on our flight, all of whom were taken off first. There, Fiona Murphy, Colin and Maureen's daughter, met us and drove us 400km to Durban, a journey of three hours through flat countryside. I was a little disappointed to see not too much scenery, only one big highway and big, big traffic. Then we entered the Natal Province, with beauty everywhere and large cattle ranches, lovely hills and valleys but, not a drop of water anywhere.

The shock of seeing Durban city and the number of black minibus taxis that were everywhere. In fact I counted sixteen people getting into one - everyplace, thick with the indigenous population. The city was bustling with activity and prosperity. Then we drove to Umslanga, where our stay was with Rob and Kathy. Rob had a great barbecue outside on the deck near the pool, with lovely views and in a lovely neighbourhood. We had a great evening talking and acclimatizing to the beautiful scenery, and temperature which was, incidentally, $2°$ in Dublin and $25°$ where I was. At bed time, the windows were left open, except for a net curtain and a small device, which can be plugged into the wall socket. That was to keep the mosquitoes away. Apparently, the 'blue chip' attracts them and fries them up.

The next day Rob announced that he was taking Colin and myself on safari, a distance of 250 miles to Mkusi Wildlife Park, (a vast tract of habitat, totally fenced and protected by wardens with guns to prevent poaching). This trip surely gave me an insight into life in South Africa. The indigenous population were everywhere. None of them seemed to have work, but all had light blue overalls, wellingtons and caps. I'm told, apparently, that *'what keeps out the cold also keeps out the heat'*. Then, it was on through Richards Bay, where Colin had worked, years previously, before his return to Ireland. He worked on the construction of the paper mill in the area. Every bit of land was under Sugar Cane in that area and lots and lots of natives were in the fields tending to it. They were mainly women, as they are the best workers. The men just stood looking, as if they were bored. As I commented to Colin about them he told me that, *"it would take four of them to replace Aiden"* (my workman at home at the time, Aiden Hegarty).

Apparently they earn very little money but they get fed by the farmer. Then, I saw forests for miles and miles, with 'shanty huts' scattered everywhere – but, I must say, all neat and tidy! Colin told me that the huts were supplied by the forestry company for its migrant workers. After the forest area we came to where the natives were selling carved articles which they had made from off-cuts of timber. They sold them to tourists, who were very plentiful still in that beautiful countryside. It was a dirt road of about fifty miles, but I never saw so many natives - men, women and minibus taxis. From Ireland to Mkusi, this is an incredible area, with so many natives walking around aimlessly. There were lots of cows and calves in this area, but not as we know them! I saw horses and donkeys in poor condition, also, hens and chickens which were kept for a meager survival.

Then the big sign for 'Mkusi Wildlife Park'. There were huts everywhere. They were built from mud blocks, which the women had made, built and thatched, themselves. The men mostly sat around and drank beer. That was the 'bush country'. Then my first glimpse of the big giraffe and a young one beside it. Later I saw Wildebeest, Zebra, Deer, the Niala, Snakes and Baboons. But the Rhino that I had hoped to see, wasn't in sight. The tourist accommodation was first class – a group of neat log cabins. I wondered who kept them so neat and tidy. Even though we had our own food with us, which we cooked, we slept 'till early morning and went on safari every day, the house was always spotless when we returned. I wondered how this happened so discreetly, as I never saw the ladies around. But, this was their way of getting on with it.

One night, as I wrote the day's adventures, the worst thunder and lightning storm struck and blacked the power out but one has to be self sufficient when on safari, the torch and the good old gas stove takes care of emergencies. The shower was no problem either, for Rob or Colin, because they had to just strip off and open the door and stand under the thatched eve. By the time I got to it the rain had lightened. Still the rainwater is hot to a temperature of up to 40°, which we experienced there. At night the temperatures dropped to a lovely 20°. Then it was up at five o'clock to experience this lovely place. As there are hundreds of miles of roads in the park, the wildlife is outstanding, and I saw the fat black pigs, with long tales. But I still saw no Rhino. All the rest that are famous in Africa were there, even the crocodile and snakes, big and small. That night we went to a 'hide' (which is a small well obscured timber structure) near a watering hole to see

128

the wild animals as they come for miles to drink the water. I must say that even the long winding path is totally fenced with the most secure large poles and very sound wire. Even the gate springs closed when you enter the path.

The next day, as we drove with Rob in his 'Jetta', in the far distance, didn't, Colin (who lived there all his life), spot a Black Rhino. When we stopped I wanted to get the photograph. It was everyone's dream when on safari. We saw six of them and one baby between the fresh and lush pastures. Suddenly they decided to come in our direction. So 'low and behold', they walked straight towards the car. Apparently the Rhino has very short sight, but if he meets an obstacle in his path he just hooks his large horn in it to get through it – all three ton of him. The calf was equal to the size of a one and a half year old bullock. What would have happened if our car did not start? I don't think I would have been able to run. As Rob reversed the car, the Rhino walked straight across the road in front of us. It certainly is amazing to see them up so close in their natural habitat. After that adventure we saw many more Impala, Grey Dyke, Monkeys, Mongoose and all sorts of wild birds, especially Vultures who are huge birds of prey. After seeing so much of this lovely place, we packed our belongings and headed for the exit at Mkusi and it surely was a dream of a lifetime.

Rural Africa is an eye opener. Survival is 'the name of the game'. Without work those peasant people plunder quite a bit. They steal largely to survive. The women do all the work and seem to be the breadwinners. I know I said earlier about some of them making and selling their crafts, but there are so many of them. I purchased some of their craftwork and I was tempted to buy a lot more items but the plane luggage had to be thought of. I said to Colin that I would spend £20.00. It was a lot at the time. But if I did, I would have a 'creel' full of lovely crafts, as they sell them at much lower prices than they ask for them at first. I spent a hundred 'Rand' (€30.00) all together and I shook hands with the young fellows and they seemed amazed as the only implements they had was a pen knife and an 'Adz' (similar to a hatchet). That is Zululand and the highway leads to Mozambique. As I liked geography at school this was it at its best. I said to my good friends, Colin and Robbie that they should set up a specialized tour company to bring Irish people who require an insight into Africa, which few get the opportunity to see firsthand.

Then it was back to the beautiful Umslanga, where all the neighbours had beautiful houses, landscaped to the maximum, with lovely large cars and 'four by four' pick-up vehicles, all securely locked. All have high security fencing and automatic entrance gates and usually have two large guard dogs inside – all for protection. They also have emergency response notices everywhere! Armed Police are on duty every few miles. My question to Colin was, "Why does the Establishment not encourage the young indigenous people to be educated and change their ways?" Colin said to me, "where would they start? - as the numbers are massive!" Nearer the city of Durban there were huge condominium blocks, which were all walled and had security men at the entrances. They are relatively safe, but sometimes not safe enough for the indigenous fellows who can scale walls and go through barbed wire fencing!

Our next big occasion on my trip was the wedding of Jill and Bernard. The visit to the 'Tux' shop and the 'Stag night' were two more hectic days. Jill and Bernard got married in a similar ceremony to at home. I wrote my days happenings and still savour them. The beautiful scenery keeps cropping up. During my journal writing of that trip I even wrote of being thankful, even with having MS, to be in my position on the 11th September, 1996, and seeing so much beauty and so many 'unexplainables' of this Continent of South Africa. We passed Archbishop Hurley's mansion. He was the man who used to write to my mother for a donation for the missions. I'm glad she sent him some, as did everybody else, and I know, firsthand, the good work still being done there by the missionaries. But, *"My mother's Bishop"*, as she called him, was not too badly off himself! I wrote my Reflections as follows that night:

"Another day! Colin and his grandson Darren took me to see Durban Bird Park. I called it 'A natural haven for birds'. It was a disused quarry which had to be abandoned because the blasting was getting too near to a neighborhood. The face of the cliff was 70ft., with an expanse of about two acres. It was full of growing trees and a lake with waterfalls and totally wired over (which reminds me of another time, when driving with Colin's daughter, Fiona, we were abreast with a huge 40ft. articulated blue truck, with closed sides and mesh over the top. I thought it was for chickens or pigs. But Fiona, who lived there all her life, told me that it was a Police truck, which takes prisoners from riot scenes to cool them off).

Another day in that part of Africa, Colin and Maureen took me to Scotborough, where they visited their former neighbours and there we went to evening Mass. After Mass everybody stands on the lovely green grass outside to chat. There they introduced me to a lady whose brother worked in Sligo. Then we talked with a Priest and he asked me where I was from in Ireland. My reply was vague. I just said, "Along the West Coast". He asked "What part?" and I said, "A place called 'Sligo'". Then, he asked me, "Do you know Ballymote?" I said, "I sure do! I was working there before I came on holidays". Then, he said, "Well! I was in Ballymote a few years ago." He proceeded to tell me that he was on a mission in Zambia with Bishop McGettrick, who came from Ballymote and they came back for his 50th anniversary. He also said he had stayed in Gurteen. There is a saying, "the world is a small place" and I'm inclined to agree with that!

Colin and Maureen also took me to see their former neighbour, Sonny and his family. When we got to Sonny's gate his daughter met us and said that her father and brother had been stabbed and they'd been rushed to hospital an hour before we came. Sonny owned a bottle store (off-license). Apparently as one indigenous fellow went into buy a bottle of wine another fellow distracted Sonny whilst the first fellow made a grab for the money in the till. He pulled a knife on Sonny's son and stabbed him a half an inch from his heart. Then Sonny grabbed his gun but it jammed and he got stabbed also. They made off in the direction of the railway station where the police captured the two of them. As the drama unfolded Sonny and his son arrived home all cuts and bruises with ripped shirts and bandages. Then they had plenty of banter with Colin and a good laugh. I thought it was all a bit scary, but things like that happen in most places there. So it's 'a gun for a gun' and 'an eye for an eye'.

Colin, Darren and myself at Durban Bird Park.

Then it was time for a visit with another neighbour. They are very nice also and dreamed about going to Ireland for a holiday. Naturally I spoke highly of it and wished Board Fàilte were paying me! Then it was time to visit Bridget and Hans and Skye in Bulwer at their experienced glider instruction school, where lots of well off young professional people spend their spare time gliding over the most beautiful, lush, hilly countryside. As I was amazed at the scenery, Hans told me he would take me on a tandem flight, but I declined the offer, and said, "The cat has nine lives", unlike myself. I want to keep the few I have left.

Then it was time to go to Howick to see Colin's brother Michael (now RIP). This route was amazing; some things tourists never get a glimpse of except from an aircraft. The villages where different tribes lived in clusters are all over the place. I asked why there was an odd big mansion amongst them. He said that the Chief lived in the big one and apparently, according to the process of acquiring a new wife, he had to provide a hut for his former wife and children. He could be the father of maybe twenty or thirty children, with, perhaps, between five and eight wives. Incidentally, Howick has the tallest waterfall in Africa and is a major tourist attraction. I saw the only stonewall of my travels there and as I had told somebody at home, who asked me why I was going to Africa, I said in a mocking way that I had, "a stone wall to build". So the photo of that wall came in handy.

We saw some very good grassland, herds of cattle and bales of hay. Also a few poultry farms and sheep and goats. Our next visit was to the Catholic Mission to see Sr. Frances Ann, a Dublin native and another young nun from Ardagh in County Longford. This was a very important stop as I had heard all about Sr. Frances Ann and the nuns there. The nuns had taught all of the Murphy girls. I never thought I would be privileged to see a Mission at first hand. This missionary scene, which I have recorded was as we all had heard and read the magazine 'Africa' and the 'Far East'. Sr. Frances Ann was the most saintly person I have ever met.

As we headed back to Durban, we passed a lot of 'chockablock' towns, full of natives everywhere. I saw a young girl with white dough on her black legs and I, again, asked Colin why this was. He replied, "She is a trainee Witch Doctor" (Siogoma). I also saw women with large car batteries on their heads while carrying two shopping bags. I said, "I must get a photo" but he was afraid she might see me and we could be in trouble.

We were 150 miles from Durban and still in the heart of rural Africa with mud huts everywhere and no hurry on anybody, but still a lot of natives in groups along the roadside, mostly women and children and a huge amount of empty bottles in wheelbarrows. I curiously asked Colin "What are they about?" and he said that they "were waiting for the 'booze lorry' to come along". Then, sure enough, didn't we see it parked on one side of a large groups of people. I notice that there were little or no men to be seen. Then, Colin told me that the men were minding the 'Shanty huts' maybe, a few miles up in the hills. They were waiting to drink all the booze when the families returned. It sure is a different culture – very different to the western world!

We were in Underberg – the vast amount of natives everywhere, I keep remarking about. Black 'Hiace' minibus taxis, the most vehicles, they all have radios and loud music, but they do not have the luxury of the spare wheel. Two or three people will carry the punctured wheel whatever number of miles to the nearest garage to be repaired and then walk back, as time means nothing to them. Once on our travels I asked Colin what were the 'make-shift' towers with ladders up to them that were in the forest and crop areas. He told me they were lookout posts to combat forest fires. The local ladies are best at the job of watch, as the men fall asleep. The important thing is that they are radio controlled.

From Howick we went to Petermarisburg, the Capital of Natal Province, to see a friend of Maureen. It was Christmas Eve and time to get to Umslanga to Rob and Kathy's in time for Midnight Mass. With the church packed and singing – the very best I ever heard - I don't think our religion is dying in Africa. Then it was time to ring Pauline and the family to wish them as happy a Christmas as I was having. Christmas Day was hot, 34°, and dinner outside on the deck beside the pool. There were sixteen in number here altogether but all talking about leaving Africa for a new life in Canada and elsewhere, which a lot of them have done since that. (Rob and Cathy and their children are just home from Canada where they are enjoying life and were here to visit me recently).

I now recall St. Stephen's Day in Durban, shopping with all air conditioning everywhere to help combat the 33° heat of the day. Even the local newspaper commented about the huge congestion on Durban beach and that the indigenous population made it a rarer scene than ever. Of course the political transformation of Nelson Mandela's government, meant human rights for all citizens and total freedom for the different cultures evidence of which is everywhere.

The Zulu Folk Village was another huge experience. The native dress that the women wore were long wraps around their waists and rows and rows of beads around their necks, but that was all. The male dancers wore long grass around their waists and a piece of cowhide below their knees, which they flapped up to protect their knees at certain parts of the dancing when in a kneeling position. The group of Zulu dancers numbered around twelve. We were told they were re-enacting a ritual of a boy looking for the correct bride.

Apparently he first looks in their eyes, and then feels their hands. There is always one who will appeal to him. He looks at her intensely before anything can progress. Then, the Witch Doctor and her assistant are called for more intense scrutiny. They kneel and throw a handful of bones which they gave the bride beforehand towards the boys and depending on the way they fall, the Witch Doctor decides which boy is suitable for her. There is great jubilation then and the tribal dancing goes on for hours, sometimes for days.

I forgot to say that the number of cows he can provide her father with determines things before he can marry her. This is another task which the Witch Doctor has to determine, also. I noticed it was an English speaking Zulu man who was the narrator. They all chant inside the thatched hut and the big drums beat outside. I can recall matchmaking in my parish, but not with so much ritual. When the commotion was over Colin and his girls got me down the hundred steps and rough ground to enjoy the wedding preparations. Two of those super fit Zulu warrior clad men were sought to get me up to 'terra firma'. They just picked me up and my wheelchair and ran in reverse with the fellow at the back facing me. They were incredibly strong and fit with no sign of sweat on them. I still have to read about Shafra, the first leader of the Zulu Army. Colin told me about the unreal discipline he imposed on his army.

Now it was the 28th December, 1996, my birthday, and time to get packed and head back to Bunnina. After one of the joys of a lifetime, on arrival home, the first thing I was told was that a friend of mine, Josie Devaney, was killed in a roof fall. It was time for me to get to his funeral. These are the ups and downs of life".

18

Carns Apparitions

On 2nd September 1985, the Blessed Virgin appeared in Carns, Culleens, Co. Sligo, about fifteen miles from where I live. The word spread quickly on that particular evening, with everybody in that field saying the Rosary. But as the crowd grew larger, and the 'main men' realized that the four young local girls, who had witnessed the apparition, could not be heard reciting the Rosary. It was Martin Wilson, (a man who worked for me, and was in Culleens, visiting his father and mother, Mick (R.I.P.) and Maureen, on the evening), who realized that I had a loud hailer. He rang me to get it "back to them at once!" The words Martin used to me were, "The Blessed Virgin is after appearing to four girls in Carns and a very large crowd is gathered and everybody is saying the Rosary, but they can't be heard" If I had been mobile (as like a year previously) I would have gone like *'a shot from a gun'*. Pauline and our neighbour Geraldine (and my godchild), were going and I sent the equipment with them. Alas, when they reached Carns, they could only get within a half a mile of where the girls were saying the Rosary, with all the people answering it. My ladies told me afterwards, that they proceeded to convey the address system to people ahead of them who kept passing it overhead 'till it reached Mick Wilson and the other men who were controlling the crowd. They duly set up the amplification and soon the Rosary could be heard as good as in Knock or Lourdes.

Devotions still continued for weeks after that and the most unreal large crowds kept coming to that field in Carns, in cold and sometimes nice moonlit nights and I visited it on many nights. I know people who had unexplained experiences, but as I am only writing my own experiences, it goes as follows: I might sometimes, get the strong *'smell of roses'* in that field and no roses in bloom to remind me of it. Another personal experience, that I cannot explain, was that even though in the month of September, we were all in an ordinary field and I never had a bit of mud on my shoes. I still go there and pray and I am happy to call to the landowner, who gave over the possession of land and Mick and the neighbours – there is a beautiful shrine there, which is as peaceful a place as any on a pilgrimage. All those thoughts are that of a simple believer, like myself, in the power of God.

As I write this account of the Apparitions in Carns I am saddened to learn of the death of Mick Wilson, one of the main men involved in helping out with the Carns Apparition and the Shrine in later days. I want to take this opportunity to pay tribute to Mick and his colleagues who worked so diligently to make the shrine what it is today.

The following piece was written by the Visionaries on the occasion of the Mass to celebrate the 21ˢᵗ Anniversary of the apparitions:

Twenty one years ago, on September 2ⁿᵈ four girls witnessed an apparition of Our Lady and St. Bernadette. On the advice of our local priest, we began a nine night vigil. On the second night, friends and neighbours gathered as news of the occurrence was travelling fast. Thirteen out of twenty people fell to their knees as Our Lady appeared. Little did we know the crowds, which were to come, would grow from hundreds to thousands by the end of the nine nights.

On the third night, Our Lady realising that we were scared and frightened, sent us someone to guide us through the years to follow.

A man stepped forward out of the crowd, and with a smiling face asked what he could do to help us. That man was Mick Wilson and it is because of him and wonderful men like him that we have this grotto you see before you. Mick was our Guardian Angel, our father figure, our chairman, our chief but most of all a friend. Long before this grotto was built, as we stood on a hill in this field, it was Mick who welcomed the crowds. Mick who gave us comfort when we were frightened. When the wind blew and the rain fell, it was Mick who sheltered us from the cold and held an umbrella over us. When we didn't know how to deal with ridicule, Mick found the right words to say.

On the 2nd August this year, once again Mick stepped forward out from the crowd when Our Lady carried him in her arms to his heavenly home. Mick may not be here in body but his spirit will live on within these grounds and his memory will live on in our hearts, because to us Mick, you always stood out from the crowd.

By
Patricia McGuinness
Colleen McGuinness
Mary McGuinness
Mary Hanley

This is the Shrine at Carns where people come to pray

19

Reflections of Life in my Latter Years

The Popes of my era always made an impression. Firstly, there was Pope John Paul II. My first memory involving the Pope was when we got married and we got a Papal Blessing from the Vatican. It was very important to have it on the day of your wedding and it was read out. As a coincidence, a lot of my generation's sons were called after him.

Another memory of the Pope was in 1981, when Pauline and I had a trip planned to Rome when He was shot in Saint Peter's Square that same week. So it meant we did not see Him. In 1979 on his visit to Ireland, and in particular his special trip to Knock Shrine, which was a major event in my lifetime, all available young men were organised by each diocese to act as stewards of the day. My stewardship proved a small bit hazardous, as I was situated in the ladies' toilet area. Alas the Pope's late arrival by helicopter, meant that my job became extra busy, controlling the queues as it started to look like a 'war zone', with handbags as the main missiles and also explicatives never heard at Knock before or since. As a result, I only got a glimpse of Him in the helicopter as it got dark – they could not fly in the dark at the time and also there was no airport in Knock.

The end of the story was when Peadar Kearins and myself were going home in the early hours of Monday morning, we had to rescue a stranded lady who frantically waived us down for a lift, only to announce to us that the first thing she was going to do when she got home was to 'kill' her husband. Apparently he went home early and left her in Knock. The last thing that I recall about Pope John Paul II is that he died when I was in hospital in 2005.

One balmy night in September 1989 good friends of ours, Tom and Margaret Kennedy, Pauline and myself attended an all night vigil at Knock Shrine. Sr. Breege McKenna, well renowned for her great gift of spiritual healing, was the guest speaker that night. The Basilica was packed so we stayed outside and listened to the ceremonies relayed with the aid of loudspeakers. At that particular time I was finding it very hard to accept my illness and was worried about the future, especially about providing for my very young family. The theme of the sermon from Sr. Breege was 'Spiritual Healing as opposed to Physical Healing – The Grace of Acceptance'.

We were standing in the courtyard at 5.00am when she rushed past us on her way to catch a flight. She turned around and came back to where we were and laid her hand on my shoulder. She said, "You will be alright" and continued on her journey. That moment was a turning point in my life, when I began to get acceptance of my illness and looked forward to the future again. I started to enjoy life and I still have that sense of well being today. God and the Blessed Lady worked through Sr. Breege that night and the grace of hope I received that night has stayed with me since.

Another great nun who had an influence on my life was Sr. Finbar (Martin) who was a member of the Mercy Order, resided in the convent in Skreen, and taught in our schools between 1974 and 1981. She was the most inspirational woman I ever met and I had the good fortune to interact with her in a lot of social activities which we started locally. First of which was the Pioneer Branch with its hilarious drama and sketches. Then the Beltra Youth Club, another major attraction, was to start up years after the community games. Thank God, she is still hale and hearty in the year 2006, and living in the main Convent in Ballina. I enjoyed a visit to her recently.

It would be impossible for me to pay adequate tribute to all the good women I have encountered down the years. Firstly, the hard physical work of the 40's, 50's, 60's and 70's and the full-time working women of this generation who work full time plus rear their families and do their housework.

One of the heroins of the War of Independence was our own Lynda Kearins who gained national prominence for her compassion and bravery throughout the struggle. A book in her honour, 'Lynda Kearins' was written by Prin Duignan and lauched in 2003 at the Mansion House in Dublin by Brian Lenehan T.D. Minister for Children. I was honoured to attend that lauch and to MC at our own local launch which was held in the Community Centre and officiated by Éamon Ó Cuív, T.D., Minister for Community, Rural and Gaeltacht Affairs, all due to the good efforts of Martina Kearins.

Pauline and myself with Seamus Clarke and Mattie Clarke
at the Mansion House launch

St. Patrick's Well, Dromard

St. Patrick's Holy Well in Dromard was always part of life in our parish and far beyond. So much so that our football club was named after it when it was formed in 1958. The nine-day devotions always start with mass said there on 29th June each year.

It was badly in need of repair when I first became ill in 1989. Naturallly, it was one of my first voluntary jobs and I was proud to restore it using the original stone altar from Dromard Church. Hughie James and his son Tom deserve great credit for their commitment down the years to maintaining the well in good condition. Shamie Donegan always brought a small bottle of holy water from the well to sprinkle on our team mates before every important game.

I proudly include the following extract from the 'Sligo Champion' of 6th July 1940 as included in the 2005 book by Roy Clements, 'Mainly Skreen and Dromard In Co Sligo'

SLIGO CHAMPION 6TH JULY 1940
'The annual pilgrimage to the Holy Well at Dromard took place last week when a very large number of people took part. The roads leading to the well were crowded and scenes of devotion and piety were witnessed at the traditional spot.'

The Total Abstinence Association that I am a member of all my life was a challenge, but a worthwhile one. The friends and social activities were always good for all of us. I know that everybody that remained faithful to it never regretted it.

Skreen & Dromard Total Abstinence Association

Standing at back, left to right; Tom James, Nigel Collery, Pat Donegan, Seamus Reilly, Sean Golden, Sean Egan, Jimmy Reilly (RIP), Edward James.

2nd row from back, left to right; Teresa Donegan, Mary Haran, Eamon Carney, Patrick Kearins(RIP)., Sarah Marley , Peggy Lacken (RIP), Anne Cuffe, Helen Kilgallen, Maura Lacken, Bernie Conlon, Gertie Mahon, Nora McHugh and two Sligo Pioneers.

Seater; Fr. Pat Munnelly, Dan (RIP), and Dolly (RIP), Farry, Anne Kilcullen, Mary Kennedy, Ellie Kelly (RIP), May Kearins (RIP),, Geraldine Kiely.

Kneeling at front; Cathal Egan, Nessa Collery, Leonie Giblin, Sr. Mary Nallon (RIP), Karen and Cathal Kennedy,, Padraig Donegan, Thomas Egan, Jimmy Kilgallon.

Like every child of my generation in the 1940's/'50, it was very important to emulate your father's political affinities. And, I was no different to the rest of them. He taught me to shout "Up Dev.!" for all callers to our home. I also remember the second ever Fianna Fail TD, Eugene Gilbride, for the Sligo/Leitrim Constituency, around election time in my home, as they discussed strategy and a canvass - all before proper 'cumman's' were organised. Road and wall slogans were the norm with one hot head or another rising the oppositions tempers. This is the way it was until the advent of radio and then television giving a total new dimension as the '60's approached.

My early involvement occurred as it happened around then at the time of the 1969 General Election, when a good-looking young fellow, whom we all knew contested the Fianna Fail seat for Sligo town as well as North and West Sligo areas. He was Ray McSharry and related to the Clarke family from Dromard, as his mother was Annie Clarke a teacher in the local Ballacutranta school. Ray used to play football with us when out on his summer holidays from Sligo.

Little did any of us know that this energetic young fellow would do us all proud as he worked his way up the political ladder and finish his political career as European Commissioner for Agriculture. He was one of the men who shaped modern Ireland to what it is today.

In the early years of Ray's political career he organised our Cummans properly and was a regular attender of all Cumman meetings in the constituency. It was wonderful to interact with him and his complete handling of democracy. I remember once as I canvassed the 'highways and by-ways' of our area with Ray, we encountered a lot of obstacles used as gates and some gates tied with bale-twine, not to speak of hungry dogs. As I commented to him that if he got elected to the new European Parliament, he would be able to sort it all out. Little did we know that he was going to play a leading role in the newly formed Commission and become an international figurehead.

One of the most compassionate and loyal men I ever met was John Greer of Dromard, our local shopkeeper and merchant. His travelling shop (large van) called at our house every week. As the '*barter*' system was the woman of the house just had to walk out to the van (in our case every Thursday) sell her eggs, buy a few groceries, paraffin oil and the cost of the eggs paid for most of the weekly shopping.

My mother had a huge rapport with John Greer and I recently got John to put a few memoirs on paper and it goes as follows;

"Just a few random notes about how people lived in these parts from the years 1925 to 1940:

I went to High Park School in 1925 and have lived all my life in this area up to the present time, 2005. I left High Park school in 1934 and at that time there was great adaptation in the area about dividing the Bunnina lands, which extended from Caltra road to near Ballinleg and from Castlelodge down to the sea. The people who owned the lands in the area eventually agreed to hand them over to be divided and then, in turn, different areas were given to different people, new houses had to be erected and all the people involved seemed to be very pleased.

It did take a long time to get all the houses and fences in order and everybody seems to be very satisfied. My father had a travelling shop business. After I left school, he took me with him on the van to learn the business. In due time I took over the business and we had a big number of customers all over the country. I continued the business until 1977 and then sold it. I am very proud to say that the new owners are doing very well there, and are still supported by the same families as we were over the years".

Signed; John Greer

John and his wife, Ina, live happily in their retirement, are 'hale and hearty' and John is still a joy to talk to.

When I reflect on all the things I've done in my life, I'm also prompted to think of some of the things I never did and here are a few of them -

I never used a fishing rod.

I never fired a shot from a gun.

I never smoked a cigarette.

I never drank alcohol.

I never climbed Knocknarea.

I never went in a boat on the sea in my local area.

I never drove a tractor.

I never used a computer.

I never lived anywhere, except in the house where I was born.

I never had a brother or a sister.

I never saw my grandfathers or grandmothers.

I was never in Lough Derg.

Prior to the showbands of the '60's, ballroom dancing and the huge tradition of country house céilis were the order of social life. I certainly remember the céilis as a child and the huge excitement in our townland when the Reynolds family and the 'Goat Skin Ceili Band' came to play in our good neighbour's home of the Kilcullen family. My memories are vivid of those times as my mother was always helping with the tea and food in the middle of the night - maybe at 2.00 am or 3.00 am. My father, who played Irish music himself, revelled in the fun. I remember it was even the start of a romance.

My later memories of the local dancehalls are numerous, but it was in the year 1962 that the 'golden sixties' took off when the massive new ballroom was constructed in Strandhill, 'The Silver Slipper'. As the showbands were getting very popular the first big opening night featured Mick Delahunty and his Ballroom Orchestra and a crowd in excess of 2,000 patrons turned out for the occasion. Alas, I was not there as the admission charge was a bit steep - £1.00 - which was a day's wages. Still I went a lot to it in the '60's. But, I seemed to enjoy more the 'Marine Ballroom' in Enniscrone and 'Seafield Ballroom' in Easkey, where I knew all the people so well.

In those early exciting times we travelled by the odd car which was always packed with a load of six or eight young people. But alas, there was very few cars so we travelled in the back of cattle lorries, calf vans and I even went in a hearse. Still, if I had *'a date'* I would cycle to Easkey and home, a distance of sixteen miles, which I knew well from my 'tech' days.

On occasions we went to other major ballrooms including, Pontoon, Bundoran, Drumshambo and Rooskey to dance and listen to the very best of bands. I want to list them here for you in memory of the good times we had;

Brendan Bowyer, Tom Dumphy and the Royal Showband	*Butch Moore and the Capital*
Dickey Rock and the Miami	*Larry Cunningham and the Mighty Avons*
Joe Dolan and the Drifters	*Eileen Reed and the Cadets*
Sean Dumphy and the Howdowners	*Brendan O'Brien and Joe McCarthy and the Dixies*
Doc Carroll and the Royal Blues	*Gerry Cronan and the Ohio*
Brian Coll and the Plattermen	*Big Tom and the Mainliners*
Frankie McBride and the Polkadots	*Muriel Day and Dave Glover*
Mickey Brennan and the Cliffoneers	*Philomena Begley and the Rambling Men*
Johnny Carroll (the man with the golden trumpet) and the Premier Aces	*The Clipper Carlton*
Margo and the Country Folk	*Donnie Collins*
Maisie McDaniel and the Fendermen	*Gerry Reynolds and the High-Lows*
Ray Lynam and the Hill-Billies	*Jim Toban and the Fire House*

Apart from the regular dance hall, we all looked forward to the annual carnival. This was a two week long festival of dancing held in parishes and villages throughout the country to fund raise for local projects. The carnivals were held in local flat field under a four or five pole canvas markee. The markee and the surroundings may have been simple and primitive but the maple floor was always top quality and laid down in sections to facilitate the excellent ballroom dancing fraternity. The brilliant fun we had could never be surpassed at the ballrooms and is recalled vividly by my generation. Huge crowds of patrons travelled from miles around to enjoy the guest artists and the showband music and *'interact'* with the host community. Unlike our football rivalry, this is where many a romance prospered.

The Clancy Brothers & Tommy Makem, The Dublin City Ramblers, The Dubliners and others were popular on the cabaret scene. We were also lucky enough to see and hear Jim Reeves, Johnny Cash, Adam Faith and Slim Whitman.

At the end of each night's entertainment, the band played our National Anthem and we stood to attention. The 'compere' would finish out the evening with these words, *"Good night, God bless and safe home"*. Those happy memories are all etched in the minds of my generation.

I would like to record some commonly used everyday *'sayings'* from my younger life in my locality that may not be so well used nowadays, but I want to acknowledge their value for posterity;

The longer you live, the more you learn	*It's not what you know, its who you know*
The truth can be blamed but never shamed	*Don't kill the goose that laid the golden egg*
He who is free from sin, let him cast the first stone	*If you sleep with dogs, you rise with fleas*
A stitch in time saves nine	*A burned child dreads the fire*
It's as well to be hung for a sheep as for a lamb	*You don't throw the child out with the bath water*
A picture painted counts a thousand words	*A problem shared is a problem halved*
If one throws enough mud it is bound to stick	*Never put off until tomorrow what you can do today*
He who hesitates is lost	*What's for you won't pass you by*
He/she was dressed to the (door) knocker (the finest piece of decoration on your house)	*You can bring Mohammed to the mountain but you can't bring the mountain to Mohammed*

Two heads are wiser than one even if they are only sheeps heads	You cannot teach an old dog new tricks
You cannot put an old head on young shoulders	If you have not got a horse you must plough with an ass
There is no point having a dog if you have to bark yourself	The new broom sweeps clean but the old one takes all the corners
You cannot whistle and eat meat	A shut mouth catches no flies
When in Rome you do what the Romans do	Its like looking for a needle in a haystack
A yard of a (shop) counter is as good as a farm of land	You will never know the good of the bush until it is cut
There is no fool like an old fool	He has neck for a mile of a chin
A bird in the hand is worth two in the bush	What is good for the goose is good for the gander
Rub shoulders (with friends)	You hit the nail on the head
If you dig a hole deep enough you are bound to smother yourself	What you lose on the swings you gain on the roundabouts
It takes only one bad apple in the basket to rot them	The cat has leave to look at the queen
all might cramp his style	He/she has a tongue as sharp as a razor
He/she will pass themselves out they are going so fast	You can bring a horse to water, but you can't make him drink
A shine in your shoes that you can see yourself in	There is no trace or 'tidance' of him/her
He was taking the two sides of the road with him	He went through thick and thin to get here
Through hell and high water	Doctors differ and patients die
Good riddance to bad rubbish	He/she is as black as a pot
You're as far out as the light house	It's a good job and a cheap job

He would see a flea winking on Knocknarea	That's pushing the boat out a bit too far
He has eyes in the back of his head	Ballard with the evil eye
Was it the wet day the rain came?	Paddling your own canoe
Taking the bull by the horns	He has an eye like a hawk
You wonder if running or walking easy is the best	It was the last straw that broke the camel's back
If you can't beat them, join them!	If it's not broken why fix it?
There is more to it than meets the eye	He got rapped on the knuckles for saying that
He got his wings clipped	She tore the lard off him
Life is what you make it	He can do no wrong in her eyes
He is skin deep or luke warm	There are two sides to every story
There is more than one way to skin a cat	He does not know his 'arse' from his elbow
He cannot see further than his nose	His bark is worse than his bite
Don't put words in my mouth	I have been there and done that
You scratch my back and I'll scratch yours	Something small is better than nothing at all
It's an ill wind that does not blow some good	You cannot make a silk purse out of a sow's 'lug' (ear)
A half loaf is better than no bread	Hills are green far away
When it rains it pours	Spare the rod and spoil the child
Don't judge the book by its cover	You hit first and ask questions later
The fat will be in the fire	There are sour grapes there
She thinks the sun, moon and stars shines out of his backside	As cute as a fox

You knocked the wind out of his sails	He would not hit the townland he was born in
He would turn in his grave if he heard that	He would not see it if it hit him between his eyes
I'll see you when I get my glasses!	You should go-bag and baggage
It was so dark we could not see a styme	He would not kick the door even if he had a hold of the latch
You'd swear he had a hole in his hands	People in glass houses should not throw stones
Eavesdroppers never hear good of themselves	He came with one hand as long as the other
It's a slippery stone around a gentleman's hall door	The nearer the church the further off from God
Lightening can always strike twice	The hungry eye sees far
If you cannot do someone a good turn, don't do them a bad one	You should dangle a carrot in front of him
kill two birds with the one stone	He gave her the cold shoulder
You cannot draw blood from a turnip	It would be like bringing coals to Newcastle
Smile and the world smiles with you, cry and you cry alone	If I had a penny everytime I heard that one I would be a rich man
A rolling stone gathers no moss	That should soften his cough
To run with the hare and hunt with the hound	When God made time He made plenty of it
One after another like sheep going through a gap	When you fall into a bed of nettles, it's difficult to know which one stung you
The world is a small place	Wound up like a gramophone
What you don't know won't trouble you	As cross as two clocking hens tied together
There's more fish in the sea than will ever be caught	Sometimes, you have to be cruel to be kind

It was not from the wind he took it	*Empty vessels make most noise*
It's a long road that hasn't a turn	*Its far off what God sends*
He talks 'ramais' (nonsense)	*He is just a leather lugs*
Actions speak louder than words	*Let it in one ear and out the other*
You're as well spilling water into a leak'n' bucket	*They are as different as chalk and cheese*
There is no point beating about the bush	*There are more ways to choke the cat other than with butter*
He would drink it out of a sow's trough	*How would you feel if the shoe was on the other foot?*
There is no point throwing the cat among the pigeons	*Look at the head he has on him and the price of turnips*
I need to put on my thinking cap	*Beauty never boiled the pot*
All picture and no sound	*He threw boiling water on it*
He's as thick as two planks nailed together	*Speak of the devil and he's sure to appear*
There's no fireside like your own	*Speak of an ass and he's sure to pass*
You should be thankful of small mercies	*When you're standing in a doorway your neither in or out*
He would swear a hole through a pot	*Swear on your mother's grave*
That's the long and the short of it	*This is the end of the road for me*
As water tight as a duck's 'arse'	*Hold everything even your breath*
I wished the ground would open up and swallow me	*An empty bag won't stand up and a full one won't bend*
You're carrying a lazy man's load	*Two swallows never made a summer*
*He would not give you the steam of his p**s*	*I'll be there in two shakes of a lamb's tail*

There's no flies on him and if there are they are dead	She died like a chicken (all of a sudden)
The world and his wife knows it	I went around the world for sport
As blind as a bat	As straight as a dye
The sky is on the ground	Look at the gimp of him
Two wrongs don't make a right	As crooked as a ram's horn
He/she is a cuckoo (only child)	There is never smoke without fire
She's like a turkey walking on stubbles (what's left in the field when the crop is harvested)	When God made you he threw away the mould
As thin as a wisp	Not the length of my big toe
The squeak of a field mouse	There's method in my madness
You were as well singing as crying over spilled milk	An apple a day keeps the doctor away
Trying to make ends meet	Hanging on for dear life
Attack is the best form of defence	You have to listen to thunder
The least said, the easiest mended	Take it with one hand and give it back with the other
The Devil you know is better than the one you don't!	Never push your granny while she's shaving
A pessimist always says, "the glass is half empty" and an optimist will always say, "the glass is half full"	
Keep her lit!	

When a man wanted to *test the water* for a marriage proposal with his sweetheart, he might humorously use some of these old sayings:

How would you like to have your shoes under my bed?
How would you like to be buried with my people?

If a death was pending people might be heard to say:

I think he will be 'sleeping out' fairly soon.
He's 'twenty for out' (as used in the card game '25')
He'll be 'shooting up the daisies' fairly soon

If you came across a bad whistler or singer you might comment like this:

If you had a string you could tie it (your mouth closed)
Can you sing far away and the further away the better?
If you had an air for it you could sing it!

My father had some sayings of his own. Even though he died when I was still very young, I remember his sayings well:

There is only one way to do a job and that is the right way
A job half done is not done at all.
It's the bit you eat that does you good, not the bit you leave after you
He might as well be looking into a whin bush
If you cannot whistle and can't play music you are no good to man or beast.

In the building trade we had our own few sayings to describe our work:

If it doesn't draw smoke it will draw tears (a blocked chimney).
If it does not draw water it will draw money *(a rushed waterpipe job)*
It's wonderful the works of a wheelbarrow, especially the front wheel

Below I have listed some Irish words that are in my dialect handed down to me and my generation but are no longer or seldom used in everyday conversation in Sligo today.

Amadan:	*A daft talkative person*
Bladderer:	*Someone who talks a lot*
Bacóg:	*An armful of loose material*
Boochalaun:	*Ragworth (yellow weed in pasture)*
Beasum:	*A handful of heather or similar tied together for whitewashing*
Bachadie:	*Lame, describing someone with a limp*

Boithrín:	*Narrow lane usually grass growing in the middle*
Birtcheen:	*Small amount of fodder carried in a rope on your back*
Bruteen/Brusie:	*A dinner of mashed potatoes mixed with butter*
Comhither:	*A spell or confusion on somebody*
Curragh:	*A wet marshy area of land*
Crocaun:	*A prominent small hill easily identified*
Ceolain:	*A saying to describe a thin light young fellow*
Conny:	*Someone nice and methodical*
Cushlamochree:	*Endearment – the pulse of my heart*
Ceanabawn:	*A bog flower or bog cotton*
Crubeen:	*Hoofs of pigs or donkeys*
Colleen:	*A young girl*
Craddains:	*A big rough weed with large conifers*
Dallog:	*A blindfold for the eyes*
Dracaigh:	*A wet misty day*
Drisheen:	*A pig's organs boiled and used as a dressing*
Donny:	*A weak bonam*
Eejit:	*A daft person who usually says and does the wrong things*
Guban:	*An unskilled workman who would chance any job*
Gasùr:	*A young boy*
Gibrish	*Talking foolishly*
A gimlet:	*A small tool for making holes in leather*
A gansey:	*A wool jumper*
A glugger:	*A hatched egg when on inspection by candlelight has not developed to embryonic stage*
Gunterer:	*A person who is an untidy and slobbery worker*
Lauaigh:	*Friendly or good natured lady*
Ludarman:	*Similar to an eejit*
Luchaun:	*A small lake less than an acre in size*

Meitheal:	A group of workers gathered together in days gone by to save crops and turf etc.
Mairhin:	The boundary fence between farmers
Mearing:	Your small finger
Mearacan:	A thimble used when sewing
Oinseach:	A young person who has an old head on young shoulders
Poheens:	Very small potatoes picked as fodder boiled for pigs
Praties:	Potatoes
Plamais:	To butter someone up
Pisin:	A kitten or small cat
Pardrog:	A creel with a detachable bottom from manure transfer
Ramais:	Gibberish
Ranai:	Delicate or thin person
Rickle:	A small narrow stack of turf
Riddle:	A sieve of various gradients used to grade sand
Rak:	A comb, also a hanging unit to hold plates or other items
Rake:	A hand tool used to grade soil or gather grass etc.
Runt:	The smallest of the litter
Scollop:	A sally rod used in roof thatching
Seach:	A thorney bush
Slaan:	A turf spade
Skillet:	A round cast iron pot used for cooking
Slough:	A large swallow of water
Sprawn:	A caked residue on the eye on awakening
Spawg:	A big clumsy foot
Scelp:	A indiscriminate slap
Straois:	A grim or unkindly face expression
Scraw:	A cut sod of grass and clay attached and allowed to dry, used as cover before thatching
Scalteen:	A half one of hot whiskey

Skieluan:	*Selected cuts of potatoes which are prepared to plant as seed for a new crop*
Scutch:	*To clean the chaff or loose leaves off grain*
Skitt:	*Poking fun out of someone*
Sacassia:	*A pet name for a child*
Strollop:	*A fat lazy woman*
A struthan:	*A stream*
Shaugh:	*A valet between ridges*
Stokous:	*An impromptu dance and celebration when an newly married couple would arrive home*
Steepeen:	*A handle with a pointed base used to make holes in soil to plant potatoes*
Stooke:	*A method for gathering and drying sheafs of oats, wheat or barley*
Tra hook:	*A tool used to wind hay ropes*
Thalogue:	*A pain in the wrist acquired from constant use*
Trainin:	*A field of pasture grass with tall stems with seed on them*
Tag:	*A short jacket or coat*

English speaking terms used regularly

Whisht:	*Hold your silence*
Whipper snapper:	*A jumped up smart alec*
Will o the wisp:	*Trim*
Waffler:	*No sense to the chat*
Yob:	*A bully boy*
Yahoo:	*More of a simpler bully*

An unknown author has described our world like this:

We have taller buildings, but shorter tempers,
wider freeways, but narrower viewpoints.
We buy more, but enjoy it less.
We have bigger houses and smaller families,
more conveniences, but less time.

We have more degrees, but less sense,
more knowledge, but less judgement,
more experts, but more problems,
more medicine, but less wellness.

We have multiplied our possessions, but reduced our values.
We talk too much, love too seldom, and hate too often.
We've learned how to make a living, but not a life.
We've added years to life, not life to years.

We've been all the way to the moon and back, but have trouble
crossing the street to meet a new neighbour.
We've conquered outer space, but not inner space.
We've cleaned up the air, but polluted the soul.
We've split the atom, but not our prejudice.

We have higher incomes, but lower morals.
We've become long on quantity, but short on quality.

These are times of tall men and short character, steep profits
and shallow relationships.
These are times of world peace, but domestic warfare, more leisure, but
less fun, more kinds of food, but less nutrition.
These are days of two incomes, but more divorce, of fancier houses,
but broken homes.
It is a time when 'there is much in the show window and nothing
in the stockroom.'

Whoever that writer is, he or she has described us well. Has a generation ever needed role models more than this one? Has there ever been a generation more in need of people who will set good example?

Many years ago when I was working on a construction site, grit got into my right eye. Immediately I started to rub my eye in an effort to shift it but with no results. I continued on rubbing it for the next few days but my eye got worse and worse until it became photosensitive. It came to a stage that I couldn't see out of my good eye, then I started to worry! I went to an eye specialist and he put a few drops in it and covered it with a pad to be left on for a couple of days. Luckily, for me a good local man Peter Davis who saw my situation told me where to go. A Rathlee woman had the cure and he told me how to get there. Posthaste I got Pauline to drive to her house for the cure. Sure enough the good lady was there and well used to fellows like me come to her in similar predicaments As it turned out I knew her son-in-law Anthony Lenaghan who happened to be there that evening. We sat down in the living room to chat. The good Mrs. Mucklehoney took a saucer of water and I proceeded to the other room with it. As I was chatting to Anthony, I felt relief coming to my sore eye but thought nothing of it. Then about 15 minutes later Mrs. Mucklehoney reappeared from the other room with the saucer of water in tow and said *"whatever was in your eye had a bad taste in it!"* I could not believe the great relief I had already. She simply said that if she had a bit of cloth belonging to me she would have been able to give me the same good result. She showed me the saucer of water and sure enough the proof was in the pudding! Floating on top of the water was a film of oily scum, which she informed me was the ointment the doctor had used, lying on the bottom was the offending article that ulcerated my eye - the grit from the site! Well I was so impressed I asked her not to throw out the contents of the saucer and called in Pauline to witness it herself.

Mrs Mucklehoney's cure was 100% successful and my eye recovered perfectly. I'm glad to say that the good lady passed down her cure to her daughter.

Another cure that always worked for me was the cure for the sprain, given by Dolly Farry (RIP) on us young fellows that had a lot of injuries due to football. She rubbed it and prayed over it. I made three consecutive visits to her in daylight and that was the end to the pain!

As I ramble along on my scooter on the main Sligo-Ballina road and observe all the rural scenes in my view, I have to mention the mile-stones that pedestrians, cyclists and horsemen were guided by many years ago.

Strategically placed milestones were used to show the distance between Sligo and Ballina. Today the chiselled insertions cannot be detected. They were gouged out by the locals, so that the Black and Tans would become disorientated as they cavorted around the countryside.

More happy memories from a bygone time as our good neighbour
Michael Boland moves my cattle to graze on more lush pasture in the 1980's

My reflections on unusual occurrences are numerous. But, too many of them told consecutively distort readers into a different interpretation of the scribe (*as of nowadays*).

Back Row from left: Ann Campbell, Ann James, Beatrice Dowd, Edel Kearns (Secretary), Ann Kearns, Philis McDonagh, Thomas James, Hughie James, Frances Murray, Pat Rush, Martin Wilson (Chairman)
Front Row from left: David James, Mary James, Molly Rush, Colie Campbell (President R.I.P.), Eamon Carney

'Cassie' and myself with my Leitrim People's Association Award , The Michael Higgins Memorial Trophy, which I received in 2001. The Trophy is awarded annually to individuals in recognition of charitable work done in the Community

20

My Home Place and Local Poetry

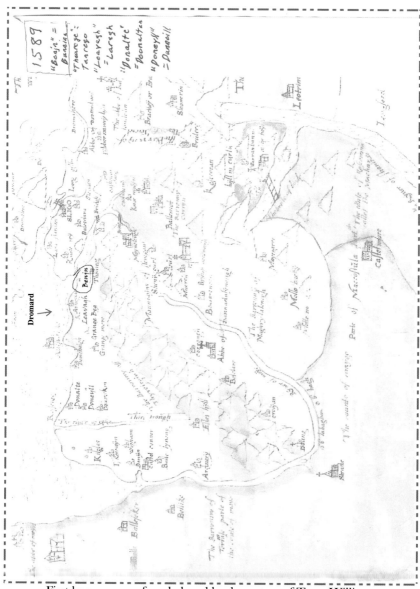

First known map of my beloved land courtesy of Terry Williams
and Sligo County Library

Now, as I sit and write in my conservatory, I'm able to survey one of the most glorious parts of our countryside – the Ox Mountains in the distance behind the lush land of Dromard. As I turn my head northward I can see the beauty of Ballisadare Bay, Strandhill, Rosses Point, round to Lissadell, Mullaghmore and Raughley Head and the Blackrock lighthouse.

All the places I've mentioned, with the exception of the Blackrock lighthouse, were visible to the early settlers in Ireland. My personal regard is with those early settlers when they chose the site of the big Motte adjacent to my land. The Motte is sited precisely in the most symmetrical position to give full vantage to those early settlers of the entire countryside from all angles, especially Knocknarea and Queen Maeve's grave. A slight move in any direction will distort its magnificent contour. I feel this would have been a significant factor in choosing the site. As I have mentioned earlier this is the only Motte of its type in County Sligo and is fairly well documented.

My view of Sligo Bay and Rosses Point from Portavade with Lissadell and Benbulben in the background

THE ELSINORE

Ye lads and lassies of the dancing classes
Ned Kelly was a roaring from shore to shore
From hills and highways and roads and byways
That followed Andy to the Elsinore

The road was blocked with cars and busses
From Juggins jibbing to Peter's pound
There was great alarm but they did no harm
They were well conducted by the great McGowan

He was hale and hearty at every party
That was ever given by Lady Gore
He hoist a flag on her Tarmen Castle
And did forty days in dark Crannmore

At Raughley Harbour a boat was chartered
To cruise to Sligo with Andy's band
Surely he'd be admired by foreign captains
When he sounds his trumpets at the Metal Man

All night long the small boats were passing
From Coney Island by the Metal Man
There were lads and lassies
With carts and asses

And Peter Jordan in his private van
The hall was full of all creeds and classes
Of dancers dancing some knew not how
But Austin Gillan got every shilling
The hens are laying in Maugherow

By James Currid
Given to me by John Joe Herity

SLIGO BAY

All Ireland o're, I do adore, still my thoughts more fondly stray
Where the white waves break along the shore of dear old Sligo Bay
For there my youthful days I passed in a cottage by the shore.
Where I heard the tempest raging blast mingle with the ocean's roar.

And often on a foggy misty night before the sun's first beaming ray
Persuade the lingering shades of night across the tranquil bay
I've seen the fisher folk embark in each small but well trimmed boat
And heard the first note of a lark who o're me in the air did float

And when the sun came rising o're Benbulben's holy crest
I watched the white waves sweeping around the rocks where the
sea birds nest
Or watch a ship come drifting in with a light air from the west
And heard her crew some yarn spin when at anchor she would rest

The sun shone brightly o're the top of Knocknarea
I watch the tide ebb quietly from the rocks where the shellfish stray
Or where some fish were playing watch, the seagulls madly flock
Or see a trawler strain when it couldn't reach the dock

As the suns warm rays were beaming as o're the waves they spread
A silvery path was gleaming across to Aughris Head
And in the boat house shadow I heard some old fisherman, his
life's adventures tell
Or watch a rainbow try to span the woods of Lisadell

And the sun was sinking on the oceans heaving breast
And the evening star was blinking where clouds glow in the west.
It was sweet to stand on Johnsport's strand
or Raughley's wave washed shore
Or where true lovers go hand in hand on the green lands of Bomore

Then the moon came rising o're the valley of Glencar
And the harbour lights were burning bright each like a little star.
It was sweet to glide with the ebbing tide and a light air in the sail
And watch the coast line gently hide in the evening's darkening vale

And often on a cold dark winters night I was wet by the spray of the gale
As I watched the numerous phosphorous lights or listen to the seals lone
wail
That is why my heart does lie and my thoughts do fondly stray
Where the white waves break along the shore of dear old Sligo Bay

By John Herity

THE CANON' S DREAM (The Boys of Ballisodare)

A dreadful dream I fain would tell:
I thought I'd died and 'woke in Hell!!!
And there, upon the topmost landing.
Some prime Collooney "boys' were standing.
Then, gazing 'round, I wonder'd where Dwelt
the "scamps" from Ballysodare.

Musing thus, I scanned each face
And from, within that dreadful place,
Prisoners of every nationality.
Therein confined for their rascality.
My quest was vain: they were not there,
The rowdy "Rakes' of Ballysodare.

Descending then, a winding stair,
Thro' sulphur fumes and horrid glare,
I searched all 'round the lower story,
'Mid grinning friends and sinners hoary.
I saw some 'sparks' from Dromahaire
Not one as yet, from Ballysodare.

A batch of captives, lately arrested.
The Squire, 'Old Nick' of that district congested.
With propriet'ry air, forthwith drove in,
'Mid clanking chains and doleful din.
They came from Sviinford and Aclare,
But no 'young blood' from Ballysodare.

"Sir Nick," quoth I, on every hand,
"I see your spoils from earth's fair land;
No doubt they well deserve their fate
Poor wretches, sad and desolate.
But might I ask you, is it fair
To quite pass over Ballysodare?"

"It owned the worst of reputations
For "loafing," poaching and potations.
Has it, perchance, escaped your toils,
While venial sins your fire assoils;
Enmeshing others, do'st thou spare
The blustering 'blades' of Ballysodare?"

"Ha! Ha!," quoth Nick, with sinister mirth.
"There's not a place on all the earth,
Exempt from my bold operations;
Resist, who can, my machinations?
I'll take you lower still, and there
You'll find the 'bucks' from Ballysodare."

Traversing hot and lurid tunnels,
Past myraid smoke-embelching funnels.
He showed me 'chain-gangs', grim and sad
Arriving there from Emlaghfad,
From Skreen, Dromard, and everywhere,
Except elusive Ballysodare.

Still down we went to lower regions,
Encompassed by perspiring legions
From Straid, Kilvarnet and Killoran,
As well as Sligo and Bundoran.
Gaunt faces wore look of worry,
Contingents these, from Tubbercurry.

At length, we reached a dungeon rude,
In Limbo's lowest latitude,
An there, I saw with apprehension,
A saucepan grim, of vast dimension,
Upon a roaring furnace boiling,
While stoking Imps around were toiling!

With conscious pride, Old Nick drew near the huge utensil.
In the rear I peer'd, with horror o'er his shoulder,
Despite the heat, my blood ran colder!
He raised the Lid, and said, "In there
I boil the 'ho'rs' from Ballysodare"!

"In vain, betimes, I tried cremation,
But such a state of saturation was theirs.
With Bass and Guinness drenched,
My fiercest fires they always quenched,
And so I boil the 'brands' in there
Who 'sow wild oats' in Ballysodare"!!!

Unknown Author
Given to me courtesy of Alfie Gallagher

The Mound of Queen Maeve's Grave on Knocknarea

A View from Saltport, Beltra as visualized by the Author of the poem 'Saltport by the Sea'

SALTPORT BY THE SEA

Farewell, Farewell, old Saltport shores, that seem so dear to me
As I wandered around you all day long, my heart was full of glee.
The prechaun dubh and the cute curlew, they had no fear for me.
They claimed that as their native home, Old Saltport by the sea.

How I gaze all day at Knocknarea, just right across the wave.
It's lofty peak, I'd like to seek, where rests our good Queen Maeve.
Can't walk across, so there's the loss, as life is dear to me
So I'll ne'er repent but rest content, at Saltport by the sea.

I'm in a maze while I wait and gaze, to hear these gathering guns
Those breakers roar, far from the shore,
you'd hear at George McMunn's
The feathery foam, is the petrel's home, oh, what a life long spree
Can live and thrive, and swim and dive, at Saltport by the sea.

But now alas, my dream is o'er, I bid a sad adieu,
Old Saltport shore I'll see no more
And far famed Carnadoo, and Culleen - a - more - a vale - astore
I'll often dream of thee, 'till my bones shall rest,
far from the West, at Saltport by the sea.

The bashful sea nymphs, blush with shame
I'm staying there so long.
But they little know by staying so, I'm writing them a song.
They'll bid me quit, I must exit, As their pleasure I would spoil
To ease their ire, I must retire, to my native Town of Boyle.

Unknown Author
Given to me by James Flanagan, Saltport, Beltra (aged 65 years)
by Ballinlig NS in the Schools Manuscript Collection
of 1937-38 Ballinlig NS. Vol 5. 168, pp. 344-5.

THE DROWNING AT AUGHRIS 1902

Come listen for a while and I'll sing to you a song,
It's of a mournful circumstance, it won't detain you long,
Concerning a sad accident that occurred upon that day
In which two young men lost their lives, not far from Aughris quay.

The sun was shining brilliantly, the day was wondrous fair.
Into that famous bathing place, young Connor did prepare.
The tide was out, he plunged about in all his youthful cheer,
And little was his notion that death it was so near.

'Til going in beyond his depth, his cries did ring the air.
And soon the brave McDermott to save him did prepare.
He never wore a medal, though many a life he saved,
But the drowning lad caught hold of him,
And pulled him beneath the waves.

If you were on the beach that day and see that sad sight there.
Connor's poor aged mother as she wept and tore her hair.
McDermott's orphaned children in grief and woe did shriek,
When they gazed upon their father's form stretched lifeless on the
beach.
God help his wife and little ones left on this earth to mourn,
A husband mild, a father kind, will nevermore return.

Unknown Author
Given to me by Molly Mahon, Farnaharpy

THE FISHERMAN

They sailed afar o'er the outer bar
When the sea and the sun light laughed
But now the storm is rising
And in light ore the great world sinks

There is a sad old rest on her weary breast
Will ye come home she thinks
For the winds and the waves are fickle
And certain fait decree

For lonely lives' have the weary wives'
Of those who sail the seas
The kettle is merrily singing
The chamber cheery and gay

The firewood rays as the others would blaze
As the cat and her kittens are playing
And baby at last is sleep
With her two little fists double tight

While the pale face still at the window sill
Watches out at the stormy night
Oh it is the gleam of a lantern
Low like a cloud faced star

How seemed then lost
Under drifting shadows afar
But it swings and springs on the water
Like only a ship's light can

And the fisher's wife has found new life
In the coming of her good man.

Unknown Author
Given to me by John Joe Herity

View of Motte and Knocknarea from my field

We have all heard about the fairies and the non-destruction of their Forts and Raths. If one attempts to destroy any of their pathways, it is not lucky. I recall my attempt to remove soil from a double ditch on my land, which is incidentally, at right angles to this large Motte. I required extras soil for my garden and I thought *"why not get the digger man with his machine"* to dig from the aforementioned *'double ditch'.*

But low and behold, his machine would not start on the appointed day as a pipe had burst and a replacement could not be acquired anywhere. As a few days passed by with no hope of getting his machine repaired, Jeff, who was an Englishman, reflected along with me and after discussion we decided to never attempt to dig the ditch again. It is 5ft. high by 10ft wide and made of clay with cockleshells mingled through it (Shell Middens), leading to a marshy area of land adjoining my property.

My opinion is that the Motte builders constructed the double ditch in order to carry the clay from the ground via this route to construct the massive Motte, which obviously, was their main stronghold. The end of the story is that I got clay from our neighbour who would not take a Euro for it in return.

To the west of where I sit lies my neighbouring parishes of Tireragh – Skreen, Templeboy, Dromore West, Easkey, Rathlee, Kilglass Castleconnor and Enniscrone. The poetry that has always enthralled me of these areas are recounted below for the reader.

THE LOVELY VALE OF SKREEN

Have you ever been to Sligo, have you ever been to Skreen,
Have you ever been to Farnaharpy, where the grass is evergreen.
Have you ever been to Aughris, where Atlantic Breakers run,
Or have you ever listened to the "roaring Corra-dun".

When Nature was dispensing her gifts with lavish grace,
She looked for lasting beauty, and found this verdant place.
Beside the rugged mountain, she planned this lovely scene,
And named this crowning mantle, "The Lovely Vale of Skreen".

She decked the plains with blossoms, the beach with golden sand,
Made silvery wavelets ripple, along Dunmoran strand.
Though beauty reigns in places, and gorgeous sights are seen,
In truth there's none that can surpass, "The Lovely Vale of Skreen".

When life's long strife is ending, and resting time draws nigh,
When youthful aspirations have long since passed me by
I'll have the consolation of knowing I have been,
In nature's earthly paradise, "The Lovely Vale of Skreen".

When mounting years beset me, and active life is o'er,
When life's pulsating pleasures excite my heart no more,
It's then I'll fondly cherish, the memories of the sheen,
And happy hours I spent within "The Lovely Vale of Skreen".

By Owen P. Melvin

FARNAHARPY FAIR

It's well I remember old Farnaharpy fair.
That was our one and only monthy thrill,
The vendors calling out their wares, inviting all to buy,
In fancy I can hear their pleading still.
I yet can see the "Whiskey Tents" and farmers shyly steal
Inside the cosy, darkened tent to celebrate a deal.
I yet can see some curious men still gather all around
And hear them urge two dealing men to 'split another pound!'

As bargains reached their climax, excitement quickly grew
And dealers slapped each other's hands with all the strength they knew.
The harness-men display a rope, the farmers to exhort,
Insisting that the rope is long, though actually it's short.
There's bridles and halters, there's reins and tethers too.
There's also cures for every ill a farmer may come through.
There's lots of embrocation for every ache and pain,
and some mysterious lotions to 'nerve' the timid swain.

Sometimes if we were lucky and had some pence to spare
We gathered 'round the candy stall to see the 'goodies' there,
And then with great abandon decided what to buy,
But often had to change our choice - the price was far too high.
Yet still we were all happy without a thought or care,
'No person could be sad at heart at Farnaharpy fair.
You'd meet with your neighbours there and possibly a friend
Who'd treat you to a lemonade and give you pence to spend.

The good old days alas are gone - new methods take their place,
But memories of the monthly fair they never can efface,
The lowing of the cattle and the bleating of the sheep,
The squeals of little piglets lie in my memory deep.
Then when the fair was over and people homeward bound,
We all resumed our placid lives 'til next fair day came round.
'Mid all life's great attractions how gladly I would share
Another day, with all my friends, at Farnaharpy fair.

By Owen P. Melvin

This poem illustrates the wit and ingenuity of some of our local characters. It was written about our Skreen 'Hill' area and given to me by Johnnie Frank Mahon, one of the wonderful men that I have encountered.

THE MOUNTAINS OF DOONFLYNN
Air : The Bold Fenian Men.

It was on the Doonflynn mountains on the tenth day of May,
The sheep owners and their dogs they gave a great display.
They rounded up the horneys and they took a firm stand
Saying "We'll make those grim invaders keep off forbidden land".

It was organized by Paddy, he is the well known quack
And Jack Rooney who lately sold a cow and had to take her back.
They were rounded up by Jimmy Tailor, Pakie Kearins and Johnny Frank
All looking as big and prosperous as the Munster and Leinster banks

The horneys pleaded innocent in decent, loud and clear,
Saying "Gentlemen of honour, we know no border here.
And in the lambing season we are inclined to roam,
So do not be too hard on us we have strayed from home".

Then out stepped the spokesman and he began to talk
Saying "Innocent or guilty with us you'll take a walk
They drove them down to Paudy's and sorted out their brands,
And sent for the owners with stiff and stern commands.

Tommy Goulden was first on the scene, he was bent low with shame
For having caused such inconvenience to men of their rank and fame.
"Be going" said they "or we'll end your days you'll ne'r be seen again.
You or your dirty horneys on the Mountains of Doonflyn.

Next comes Francis Healy looking pale and thin.
I hear you have some sheep in here or is it a sheep-sale?
He was told to take his own and to make no delay.
And keep them from straying on the high hills o'er.

Pat Harte was last on the list with indignation he was filled
"They have no right to take my sheep upon them there high hills.
I'll take the bus to Sligo and justice there I'll seek.
Be gach, they must leave back my sheep before they go to sleep".

So they drove them down to Pat 's hall door.
Mrs. Harte was on the street.
She says "You all are welcome, to see you is a treat.
Put the sheep into the paddock and then come in for tea.
My husband is at the funeral and he '11 soon be home" says she.
"Ah, thank you, Mam", says Paudy, "but we cannot delay,
Because I'm weary wandering on yonder hills today.
My poor old bones are aching, my feet are swelled with pain".
He was puffing like the engine of a locomotive train.

Big Maguire stood upon a rock reviewing the scene.
"Such crazy men as those" he said "since the floods were ever seen.
I 'm raising sheep these eighty years among my fellow-men.
Ah, God be with old Ireland and the Mountains of Doonflynn".

Composed by the man menitioned in the 6th verse
Francie Healy

180

THE MISSING DONKEY CART

It was the seventeenth of December now as the people say,
when Thomas Meehan's donkey cart that night was stole away.
When Meehan found his cart was gone, he searched Pat Kelly's shed
but on my soul, the cart was stole and an old one left instead.

Then Sergeant Dunne took up his gun when he got the dispatch,
so with four men more he started out the robber for to catch.
They traced him out the Ladies Brae into Coolaney town,
but no trace, no trail or tidings of the robber could be found.

Down in Dromard they're searching hard, they're searching night and day,
for if they catch this highway man, he'll soon be locked away,
And if no-one lived but Danny's wife, she would knock him off the line
for 'twas only a week or two before, he stole from her some wine.

'Twas on Dunbekin road he camped a little while to stay,
and from James Kilgallen and his sons their donkey stole away.
It's the truth you know and each man knows, the truth you can't deny,
that they did not know their donkey as he slowly passed them by.

When night came on he made a move when everything was still,
it took one of Manus Rowlette's sons to push him up Croagh Hill.
When he got there he took great care, he did not go astray,
'til he went to Ruanes' by the lake and their pony stole away.

He then turned back and he wasn't slack for he galloped like the wind,
and 'twas at the lodge he played the dodge and left the ass behind.
Then down Croagh Hill he sloped again as cute as any fox
and Owen McGee kept listening as he hammered on the box.

He lit his pipe and then set out for he found himself in peace,
and went from Henry Culkin's wife he stole turkeys, ducks and geese.
'Twas on Gleneasky road he went, of there he had no dread,
For passing by the workhouse the guards were all in bed.

Some Dromore men must feel so proud of what they did next day,
when six of them in an excursion car they passed him on the way.
When they overtook the robber he jumped in a field,
and one of them made the smart remark "he has Edenderry wheels".

They drove along and passed him by and left the thief alone,
and never doubted who he was 'till they came to Enniscrone.
When they came back, for acting slack, sure Ruane did them blame
so two of them they did consent to follow him again.

They hired Howley's motor car saying "we'll find him now at once"
but instead of running down the thief the boys went to a dance.
He has now gone out onto Aclare where he's played a lot of tricks
when a woman shouted after him "I've an iron to get fixed",

"'Tis a job I want" the tinker cried as "I'm very much in need,
so I'll thank you for a sheaf of oats my pony for to feed".
She then obliged and stepped aside saying "your cart is very small"
"no, my friend" the tinker cried "it's the pony that's too tall"

"I had the cart and I bought the horse, they didn't suit me very well
and if I got a buyer now both horse and cart I'd sell.
There are two men more gone after him with a splendid horse and car,
and they are sure to catch him if he hasn't gone too far,

But now I've got a telegram saying the pony can't be found
and Ruane must buy another horse to plough and till his ground.
One advice I'll give to you, let the I.R.A. alone
and friend and foe, where're you go let each man mind his own.

Given to me by Nora Neilon
Pat Cogans, Kilrusheighter
Also known as "The Duke"

THE TOWER OF SWEET RATHLEE

Kind friends we meet in love tonight
All along the tranquil shore
Three thousand miles from Ireland
We may never see no more

But dearest still is Crocan Hill than any place to me
For it is my home and my native land
and they call it Sweet Rathlee
Its deeply planted in my mind these places
I have seen from Clooneenmore down to the shore
and along the road to Skreen

The lakes and roads around Templeview
where the stream outspreads the leaf
May the heavens be with you golden lane
And the tower of Sweet Rathlee
Adieu to my comrades all tis for you I will mourn
A warm heart I will leave to you for my back
I'm forced to turn and chances a one hundred to one
I never again will see my kind old friends and neighbours
Around The Tower of Sweet Rathlee

Unknown Author
Given to me by Michael J Kennedy and Jimmy Langan

As I gaze across the Ox Mountains I recall my father's great love for the song, The Hill of Knocknashee.

THE HILL OF KNOCK NA SHEE

Dreams they are uncertain, or so they seem to be
They left me with a broken heart, as you will plainly see
I dreamt I was up a hill, some lovely sights to see
I viewed the ground for miles around the Hill of Knock Na Shee

I viewed around the countryside 'till my eyes grew sore
Killoran's lovely lakes and dales and on to Carrowmore
The streams and lakes around Templehouse
So plainly I could see
I took a view of grand old Keash from the Hill of Knock Na Shee

I viewed along the mountain side 'till I came to Cloonacool
My eyes lit on the village grand, the Chapel and the school
Where first I opened my infants eyes and oft's times played with glee
'twas there I saw the light of day and first saw Knock Na Shee

I sat me down upon a bank for to rest a while
I thought I heard a female voice come whirling with the wind
I looked around and there I found a maid stood close to me
She was one of the fairy folk from the Hill of Knock Na Shee

The maid she spoke with a trembling voice
And then to me did say
"Young man your mind is wandering, but do not go away,
Foreign lands, they may seem grand, strange faces you will see,
But there's none you'll find like the true a kind
Around the Hill of Knock Na Shee

And now I am in London town, which brings to me no joy
I was born and reared in Cloonacool, on the fair banks of the Moy
But, I'll come back another day, old comrades for to see
And I'll take another ramble round the Hill of Knock Na Shee

Unknown Author

As I enjoy my respite time in Cuisle Holiday and Respite Centre at Donamon, in County Roscommon, I feel this humourous poem is apt.

IN THE COUNTY ROSCOMMON

With the hail stones and rain
I was crossing the field
On my way to the train
When I met a cailìn
And said "Do you know the shortest shortcuts into old Ballymoe[2]?"
"Oh" said I "Cailìn òg who led you astray?
I think I'll go with you and show you the way"
"Oh" said she "my poor noble
For its you I don't know
You might kiss me between here and old Ballymore"
"Oh" said he "my young lady I've never been kissed"
"Oh" said she "my poor noble
There's a lot you have missed"
"Oh" said he "I was noted for strength and for looks
I was in college and mastered the books"
"Oh" she said "your young and your handsome
But still knows you're slow
I have a husband and six children
In old Ballymore".

Unknown Author

---

[2] To the casual traveller, Ballymoe Village is not obviously within the Boundary of County Galway. Many people mistakenly form the opinion that the Village is within the boundary of County Roscommon, as did the composer of this song.

Eimear with the strange phenomenon of the only sunflower that ever grew on a strand.
This one grew on our local strand of Portavade in 2002

Sunflower on Portavade Strand with Ben Bulben in the background

21

The Last Dance 2004

This was a relatively nostalgic occasion for me which consisted of the conclusion of my memoir writing of 'As I Heard Saw and Lived It - A Lifetime'. My good neighbour Donal Kelly, who is also a progressive builder, had purchased the Corragh Dtonn pub and dance entertainment centre of years ago, where my football club Saint Patrick's used to have all their celebrations while on our 'glory years'. Donal, who was aware of our present day financial burden of running a football club, offered our committee the opportunity to have one final dance as a fundraiser. Our secretary Gerry O'Connor transferred his pub license for the night and we had a marvellous reunion. The important part of the night is that it was a huge financial success. The highlight of the night for me was that the club honoured the team that I played with and went to America with in 1974, as county champions.

For me, personally it concluded three special nostalgic occasions in my life, associated with my involvement with Saint Patrick's. My last game of football was in Gaelic Park, New York. My last game to referee was in Hartford, Connecticut. My last dance to attend was this celebration where it all started with Frank and Nancy (R.I.P.) Kilgallen (who has recently died. God rest her). They waved goodbye to us as we departed their premises on the coach to Shannon. They were guests of honour at our last dance twenty five years later.

My last team photo taken in
Yonkers Motor Inn, N. Y. 1974

A nostalgic reunion to celebrate the anniversary of **St. Patrick's** Team trip to America in 1974

Front Row Left to Right; Noel Kearins, Thomas Mahon, Pauline Carney, Eamon Carney, Michael Farrell, Mrs. Pat McGuire, Frances Kearins, Maureen Kilgallon, Declan Foley.

Back Row Left to right; Jimmy Kilgallon, Micheal Boland, Edward Rush, Nancy Kilgallen (RIP), Eamon Burke, Frank Kilgallen, Stanley Clarke, Peadar Kearins, Charlie Farrell, Micheal Kearins, Josie Boland, Johnny Kiely, PJ Clarke.

Frank and Nancy (R.I.P.) Kilgallen at
the Last Dance in the Coragh Dtonn

Micheal Kearins and myself going over old times

22

The Man In The Arena

My daughter, Eimear, who sees my efforts at my attempt to write my memoirs, gave this very important piece to me. It goes as this;

THE MAN IN THE ARENA

It is not the critics that counts
Nor the man who points out how the strong man stumbles.
Or where the doer of deeds could have done better.
The credit belongs to the man who is actually in the arena,
Whose face is marred by dust and sweat and blood,
Who strives valiantly,
Who errs and comes short again and again.

Because, there is no effort without error and shortcomings.
Who knows the great enthusiasm, the great devotions,
Who spends himself in a worthy cause?.
Who at worst, if he fails, at least fails while daring greatly,
So that his place shall never be with those
Cold and timid souls who know neither victory nor defeat.

President Theodore Roosevelt,
"The Man in the Arena" Paris 1910

Acknowledgements

I would like to thank my sponsors:
Sligo Leader Partnership Limited
Felix McHugh, Builders
Cedar Construction & Development Co. (Sligo) Ltd.

I wish to acknowledge all those who helped in many ways, namely:
Stephanie, Brenda, Ashling and
especially, Patricia Kelly of
Freelance Secretarial,
for her excellent work in bringing this project to fruition.

I also wish to thank:
Martin Coll of Red Eye Design,
Noel Kennedy of N K Photography,
Joe McGowan, Noel Mullaney,
Helen and John O'Dowd,
Kathleen Henry and Mary Kilgannon
and all the other people whose attention I claimed
during my attempts with this publication

Finally, I wish to thank my wife,
Pauline and my family Deirdre & David Williams,
Niamh, Sinead, Eimear, Paul and Fiona
for their support and encouragement throughout.